RECIPES FROM THE REFORM

A selection of recipes from the Reform Club, London

CREDITS

Text:	Craig McDonald Marshall, Alex Fulluck, Amy Crangle
Recipe design and food styling:	Craig McDonald Marshall, Alex Fulluck and Lauren Barrett
Recipe preparation:	Craig McDonald Marshall, Alex Fulluck, Artur Saavedna, Pawel Ozimkiewicz, Angelo Pirodda
Wine matching:	Giovanni de Rose, Aurelie Dufour
Photography:	Robert Reed
Design:	Cate Rickards
General Editor:	Jonathan Blanchard Smith

ISBN: 978-0-9503053-4-9

Published by The Reform Club, 104 Pall Mall, London SW1Y 5EW

Printed by MJ Group, London

Introduction

Clubs rotate around their dining rooms. Members visit for anything from a quick dinner on their own to a business lunch to a celebratory dinner with friends. At the Reform, we also hold social events from 4 to 400 people, ranging from canapés to full five course meals.

Catering for this range and quantity of people requires a highly organised staff – from the Chef and his brigade to the Cellarmaster and those in the banqueting team who do the organisation. All have been involved in the production of this book.

Our best-known Chef, Alexis Soyer, was famous not only for his cooking, but also for his cookbooks – with such names as *The Gastronomic Regenerator, Soyer's Charitable Cookery*, and *A Shilling Cookery Book for the People*, he promoted the idea of good food as as the source of good health. One of his successors, Charles Elmé Francatelli, wrote four books, of which the most famous is *A Plain Cookery Book for the Working Classes*, though to be fair he also wrote *The Royal English and Foreign Confectionery Book*. Since him (apart from a fine handwritten cookbook of Chef Bertrand of 1862 which never saw publication) no Chef of the Reform Club has produced a cookbook. We are therefore especially proud to publish *Recipes from the Reform*, the first cookery book from the Reform Club in over 150 years.

Like the Club itself, this book has been a cooperative effort. The recipes were designed by Craig McDonald Marshall, Alex Fulluck and Lauren Barrett; the superb photographs were taken by Robert Reed; and the book designed by Cate Rickards. Amy Crangle coordinated all of them and others with efficiency and good humour. All are members of the Club's staff, and have the skills, experience and dedication that makes the Reform such a source of pride for its Membership.

JONATHAN BLANCHARD SMITH
Chairman, The Reform Club

Contents

The kitchen then: building, design & Alexis Soyer

The kitchens at the Reform Club were designed by Charles Barry with the aid of Victorian celebrity chef, Alexis Soyer. The collaboration between architect and chef resulted in the most modern kitchen of its time. The influence of the chef in the design of the kitchen is evident, with 'everything contrived for the utmost convenience and ensuring the most efficient output'.

The kitchen is an example of a linear set-up. This means that the raw produce enters at one end, goes through the kitchen to be prepared and reaches the end as a ready-to-eat product. This separation of ready-to-eat and raw food mirrors modern food safety legislation and practice.

Soyer's kitchens created a sensation. At a time when the membership of the Club was less than 1,500, he welcomed – by some accounts – around 10,000 visitors to see the kitchens during his 12-year tenure at the Club. In the illustration opposite, one can see Soyer, with his trademark cap, conducting a grandly dressed couple around the central preparation area.

Soyer continually innovated. His Soyer stove entered British Army use in the Crimean War. Stoves of the same design were used until the Falklands War, when they finally left British military service as the ship carrying the majority of the remaining stoves was sunk by enemy action.

At the Club, Soyer's innovations included town gas stoves, steam powered dumbwaiters and an early form of refrigeration.

The banquets at the Reform were famed throughout Victorian England, in particular the banquet for Ibrahim Pacha in 1846. This event had forty-six different dishes, served over seven courses, including turtle soup, for which a 'goodly sized turtle of 140lbs to 180lbs' was purchased.

Soyer's dishes still survive as part of British culinary history. Lamb Cutlets Reform originated from a rather tricky member arriving late one night and requesting something different. Soyer raided the kitchen, and, using what was available, created this now classic dish. The meal rapidly became a Club favourite, with Members such as Thackeray swearing that "the Lamb Cutlets Reform were the best in the world".

Throughout his time working for the Reform, Soyer resigned and was reinstated several times. His final resignation was tended in protest to the Club's General Committee allowing members to bring guests into the Coffee Room five days a week instead of one.

Whilst working at the Reform, Soyer published six books, including *Soyer's Charitable Cookery* (1847) and *The Poor Man's Regenerator* (1848), all providing details of cheap and nourishing meals for members of society living on and below the poverty line. During the Irish Potato Famine, the Lord Lieutenant's request that Soyer travel to Dublin resulted in the creation of 'government soup', served from his own soup kitchen.

On his return to the Club, he founded soup kitchens throughout London to combat starvation in the poorer districts.

Soyer's successors (of whom, alas, far less is known than of him) kept the kitchens to his original design. Technological improvements and statutory requirements have inevitably led to changes, but many of his innovations – and the way in which he organised the kitchen – remain in use today.

In essence, the kitchens in the Reform Club are as they were designed by Alexis Soyer.

Some chefs came and went very swiftly. Some stayed for twenty years. The kitchen has always been a good place to work – looking at the biographies of Victorian and later chefs, their time at the Reform Club is invariably mentioned with pride in their biographies.

The kitchen now

The structure and organisation of Soyer's kitchen remains in place in today's kitchen. The iron support columns that feature so prominently in prints from the 1840's are still in place, though to cope with today's health and safety requirements they are clad in stainless steel. The pastry kitchen is in exactly the same place as in Soyer's time. The meat and fish preparation areas are now where the hotboxes used to be; the potwash remains where Soyer planned it. Soyer built himself a very pleasant office within the kitchen. The office remains the Chef's office today – though no longer, alas, decorated with Soyer's wife's paintings.

Today's chefs are direct inheritors of Soyer – and of all those who followed him. That is not to say everything remains the same. The steam powered dumb waiters in the main kitchens have been replaced by electric lifts, though they use the same shafts. The floor is now non-slip, rather than the old tiles; a suspended ceiling hides the extractor fan pipework and machinery; large walk-in fridges for raw foods and prepared food replace lead lined cool rooms. And we no longer allow dogs in the kitchens.

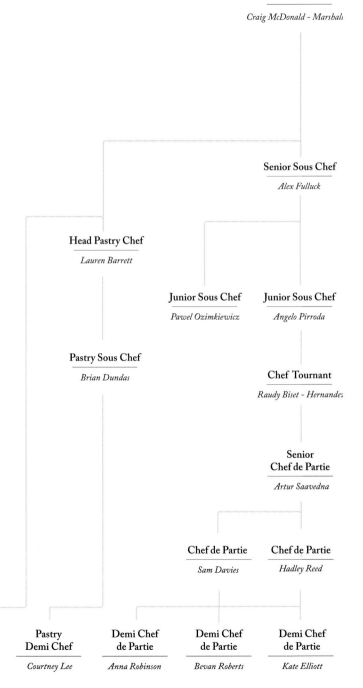

Head Chef

Craig McDonald - Marshall

Senior Sous Chef

Alex Fulluck

Head Pastry Chef

Lauren Barrett

Junior Sous Chef

Pawel Ozimkiewicz

Junior Sous Chef

Angelo Pirroda

Pastry Sous Chef

Brian Dundas

Chef Tournant

Raudy Biset - Hernandez

Senior Chef de Partie

Artur Saavedna

Chef de Partie

Sam Davies

Chef de Partie

Hadley Reed

Head Chef's P.A.

Amy Crangle

Storeman

Johnny Ram

Breakfast Chef

Maurice Kelie

Pastry Demi Chef

Courtney Lee

Demi Chef de Partie

Anna Robinson

Demi Chef de Partie

Bevan Roberts

Demi Chef de Partie

Kate Elliott

Our suppliers are carefully selected for quality, consistency and price, much as they always have been, but they now deliver into the 'goods inwards' area rather than straight into the larder. Probably much like Soyer, we strive to keep to local suppliers and ingredients from Britain.

Some of the kitchen items still in use are from Soyer's time – copper pans and heavy-based pots that we use now still bear the original Club stamp and date from the 1840's. Only last year, one of the original tables, visible in the print of Soyer's kitchen in the front of this book, was discovered in the Club's carpentry workshop and now serves in our wine tasting room.

Soyer started at the Club when he was 27. The current Head Chef, Craig McDonald Marshall, took over Soyer's kitchens at the age of 25. He worked his way up to the rôle, starting at the Club as a Chef de Partie in December 2009. Craig cites his father, who worked with Albert Roux, as 'the greatest influence on my culinary life'. The Senior Sous Chef, Alex Fulluck, is only 23 – he started working in kitchens (with the support of his parents) at 13, becoming a commis chef a year later.

These two chefs are at the head of the culinary brigade (at the Club it is still known as a 'brigade', and Mr McDonald Marshall is always known as 'Chef'). They work closely together and developed the recipes for this book. The team that works in the kitchen today is made up of 18 individuals, chosen for their drive and talent in an aggressively difficult selection process. The ages of the kitchen team range from 19 to 53, with the average age being 27.

Menus are always subject to change. Whilst the change is slower in Clubs than elsewhere, we have moved in 178 years from Soyer's complexity and innovation to 'traditional Victorian food'; to the public school food for which Clubs were once infamous; to modern French cooking (in our case a mercifully brief flirtation with Nouvelle Cuisine); to today's inspired fusion of the traditional with modern European cookery.

A Club exists to meet the needs of its Members and it is in meeting those needs that the chefs have their most difficult job. Some Members prefer the traditional food that the Club used to serve when they joined many years ago; some prefer to see the latest fashions reflected in the menu. Members arrive for a meal with friends, or may need to impress a business client. Numbers may range from one Member dining on the Long Table in the Strangers' Room at lunch, to four hundred Members and guests expecting a full, complex, dinner at the Club's Annual Christmas Entertainment.

The chefs' role is to balance these needs. Some recipes are Club favourites and remain substantially unchanged over the years – Lamb Cutlets Reform, Club Trifle, the daily carving Trolley and so on. These are the foundations upon which the kitchens provide a wide and intelligent range of modern European cuisine with a British focus.

The kitchens at the Reform are calm and industrious – there is very little shouting in the Club kitchen. One of the senior chefs is always at the 'pass' – the final step before prepared food leaves the kitchen to be taken up to be served. This ensures that there is always a moment of quality control and checking before service – so that all the work that goes into making up a dish is obvious in its presentation to the Member.

The Reform Club has operated in the same, custom made, Clubhouse since 1841. That is not the only reason why Alexis Soyer would recognise today's kitchen. He would recognise today's chefs. They combine the same passion and industry that he had, the same pride of working at the Club, and the same determination to place good food at the heart of the Club's life.

STARTERS

Smoked trout & horseradish cheesecake with compressed cucumber & dill emulsion

Serves: 6

Preparation time: 2 hrs 30 mins

For the cheesecake base

50g plain breadcrumbs
25g grated parmesan
3 tbsp melted butter

For the cheesecake topping

Olive oil (for the moulds)
150g smoked trout
500g cream cheese
50g parmesan
15g horseradish
4 eggs

Handful of chopped chives
2 tbsp lemon zest
Salt and pepper
200ml Greek yogurt

For the dill emulsion

100g dill tops
½ an egg yolk
10ml chicken stock
¼ clove garlic
100ml pomace oil
(half vegetable/half olive oil can
be a substitute)
1g xanthan gum

For the horseradish purée

1 large shallot
100g grated horseradish
1 garlic clove
1 bay leaf
Sprig of thyme
15ml white wine
40ml vegetable stock

For the compressed cucumber

1 cucumber

For serving

Fresh dill
Lemon segments
Any left over trout

The trout and cheesecake

In a bowl, mix together the breadcrumbs, 25g of parmesan and the melted butter. Press into the bottom of silicone moulds and leave to set. Chop the smoked trout. Beat the cream cheese until smooth and add the rest of the parmesan. Add the eggs one at a time, stirring throughout, then beat in the chives and lemon zest. Next, add the yogurt, and season to taste. Finally, fold in the smoked trout, gently so it does not break up further. Pour the mixture into the moulds, on top of the base, filling just over half way; do not overfill, as the cheesecake rises as it is cooked. Bake at 160°C for c. 15 mins, or until set. Once cooked, leave the cheesecakes in the oven with the door slightly open for another 15 mins, otherwise they will sink!

The dill emulsion

Put a small pan of water on a high heat. Once the water comes to the boil, blanch the dill into the boiling water and then immediately refresh straight into iced water. Make sure you squeeze the dill out really well to remove any excess water. Add the dill, chicken stock, egg yolk and garlic to a food processor and blend; then slowly emulsify the oil into the mixture. Once the mixture has emulsified, pass it through a fine sieve and then add the xanthan gum with a hand blender.

The horseradish purée

In a heavy-based pan, sweat off the shallots, garlic, thyme and bay. Once the shallots are translucent, add the white wine and cook off the alcohol. Add the chicken stock and reduce by half, then grate half of the horseradish into the mixture and cook out slightly over a medium heat.

Then transfer the mixture into a food processor. Add the rest of the horseradish and blend the mixture until smooth; finish with a splash of cream and season to taste. Remove from the food processor and leave to cool until it is needed.

The compressed cucumber

Peel a cucumber and cut it into circular slices, 1cm thick. Use an apple corer to remove the centre. Wrap the cucumber tightly in cling film and place in the freezer for half an hour. Remove from the freezer and serve.

To serve

Using a pastry brush, brush a line of dill emulsion onto the plates. Turn the cheesecakes out of their moulds and place them on top of the emulsion. Arrange the dill, lemon segments, trout pieces and compressed cucumber around the cheesecake. Squeeze the horseradish purée onto the plate at random intervals.

Salmon jellies with fennel slaw, crème fraîche & oatmeal biscuits

Serves: 6

Preparation time: 6 hrs
(including setting time; we
recommend doing the day
before the dish is required)

For the fish

600g fresh salmon
300g sliced smoked salmon

For the fennel slaw

2 fennel bulbs
25g icing sugar
15ml olive oil
Juice of one lemon
Pinch of salt

For the jelly

400ml clear fish stock
Juice of one lemon
2 bay leaves
Fennel root
(left over from the slaw)
10 peppercorns
2 sprigs of thyme
2 shallots
4 gelatine leaves
6 fennel seeds
Tiny pinch of saffron

For the oatmeal biscuits

360g oatmeal
100g flour
1½ tsp salt
1½ tsp baking powder
2 tbsp caster sugar
130g unsalted butter
200ml full milk

For the crème fraîche

200g crème fraîche
Squeeze of lemon juice
2 sprigs of dill, finely chopped
Seasoning to taste

The fish

Season the fresh salmon and bake at 170°C for
20 mins on a baking tray. Once it is cooked and
has cooled down, flake the salmon completely,
making sure no blood line, skin or bones are left in
the mix. Season and set aside. Chop the smoked
salmon into 1x1 cm pieces.

The fennel slaw

Cut the fennel bulbs into quarters, removing the
root (keep it, as you will use it for the jelly), and
finely slice using a knife or mandolin. Place the
fennel slices into a bowl and mix with the olive oil,
lemon and icing sugar. Add salt to taste. Set aside
until needed.

The jelly

Peel and slice the shallots. Put all ingredients,
apart from the gelatine, into a pan over a low heat,
and simmer gently, making sure that the stock
stays clear. If the stock goes cloudy, drop a small
amount of ice into the stock – this will cause any
impurities to rise to the surface where they can be
skimmed off. While you are simmering the other
ingredients, soak the gelatine in a bowl of cold
water. Taste the stock at regular intervals and once
you are happy with the flavour, pass it through a
sieve and add the soaked gelatine leaves, making
sure they dissolve fully. Using a ladle, lightly layer
the fish stock, flaked salmon and smoked salmon
into your chosen mould.

We recommend using silicone moulds. If you are using a single, larger mould, you should bear in mind that the jelly will take longer to set. Leave the mould(s) in the fridge to set.

The oatmeal biscuits

Combine all the dry ingredients and the butter in a mixing bowl and rub together with your fingers until the mixture reaches the consistency of bread crumbs. Add the milk and mix until a dough is formed. Remove and roll out the dough on a lightly-floured board to a thickness of around 2mm. Cut the rolled dough into shapes the same size as the moulds you are using for the fish jelly. Place the dough on lightly-greased trays. Bake for

15 mins at 180°C. Bake any extra oatmeal that you have not used, as you can use it for decoration.

The crème fraîche

Mix the lemon juice and the dill in with the crème fraîche. Season to taste.

To serve

Put a smear of the lemon and dill crème fraîche onto a plate. Arrange the oatmeal biscuits on top and place the jellies on the biscuits. Scatter the fennel slaw around the jellies with a small amount of the left over biscuits crumbled on top, along with the lemon zest and a few dill leaves.

Squash & sheep's curd cannelloni, beetroot, & pattypan squash with truffle honey

Preparation time: 1 hr

Serves: 4

For the squash cannelloni

300g sheep's curd
1 butternut squash (a ripe squash will have a bright orange inside whereas an under ripe one will be pale and not look as effective when plated)

For the beetroots

4 baby candied beetroots
4 normal baby beetroots
100ml clarified butter
100ml red wine vinegar
30g caster sugar
400ml vegetable stock

For the pattypan squash

4 yellow pattypan
4 green pattypan
(If pattypan are not available, substitute butternut squash).

For the squash purée

Butternut squash trimmings
1 shallot
1 sprig of thyme
25g unsalted butter
50ml double cream
100ml vegetable stock

For the brick pastry tuiles

3 sheets brick pastry
(available from supermarkets)
100ml clarified butter

To serve

1 small jar of truffle honey
A selection of cresses/salad leaves

The squash cannelloni

Prepare the squash by removing the outer skin. Cut the top off the squash and trim the edges so the squash is square; keep the trimmings, because you will use them later. Slice the squash into 1mm slices, preferably on a mandolin; you need 3 or 4 slices. Lay the squash slices on a tray and cover with salt for no more than 20 mins; if the salt is left any longer it will make the squash too salty. Wash the squash under cold running water and leave to dry.

For the filling, break up the sheep's curd using a fork in a small bowl and put it into a piping bag.

Next, cover a section of worktop with a sheet of cling film and rub it with a tea towel to remove any creases. Lay the squash on the cling film and pipe the sheep's curd along the edge. Roll the squash over to form a cannelloni shape.

The beetroot

Remove the stalks and leaves, and put to one side for the garnish. Wash the beetroots thoroughly. In a medium-sized pan, add the vegetable stock, red wine vinegar and sugar and bring to a simmer. Then add the beetroots and cook slowly. (This should take at least 20 mins; check throughout by poking the tip of a small knife into the beetroots;

when they are ready the knife will slide in with very little force behind it). When tender, remove from the pan and gently rub off the skins. Cut the beetroots in half to serve.

The pattypan squash
Bring a lightly salted pan of water to the boil. Blanch the pattypan for 6 mins and plunge them into ice cold water. Remove them from the water as soon as they are cold.

The squash purée
Dice all the excess squash and the shallots into 1cm pieces. Sweat the shallots until translucent; add the squash and cook for a further 5 mins. Add the thyme with the vegetable stock. Simmer until the squash is soft, add the cream and pour into a blender. Blend until smooth; season to taste. Finally, pass the squash through a fine sieve.

The brick pastry tuiles
Lay the brick pastry flat onto a chopping board and cut to your desired size. The excellent thing about this versatile pastry is that it can be baked wrapped around objects and keeps its shape once baked (here at the Reform, we bake the brick pastry whilst it is wrapped around a metal pipe to create a coil shape). Brush the pastry with the clarified butter and bake at 180°C for 3-4 mins.

To serve
Arrange all the elements around the plate with the sheep's curd cannelloni in the centre. Dot the squash purée around the plate and lightly drizzle with the truffle honey. Place the brick pastry tuile on top and garnish with your chosen cresses or salad leaves.

Pressed confît duck with foie gras mousse, cherry gel & gingerbread

Serves: 6

Preparation time:
24 hrs includes setting time
(we recommend doing the day
before)

For the terrine

4 duck legs
Vegetable oil to cover
3 shallots
3 cloves of garlic
150ml madeira
150ml sherry
100ml red wine jus
¼ of a bunch of thyme

For the cherry gel

100g cherries
1 star anise
35g caster sugar
3g agar agar

For the foie gras mousse

125ml milk
200g foie gras
100ml evaporated milk
75ml cream
½ shallot
3 peppercorns
1 bay leaf
1 ½ leaves of gelatine (as an
alternative to an espuma gun)
seasoning to taste

For the gingerbread (1 loaf)

225g self-raising flour
1 tsp bicarbonate of soda
1 tsp cinnamon
1 tsp ground mix spice
1 tbsp ground ginger
115g unsalted butter
115g treacle
115g golden syrup
115g dark brown sugar
80ml whole milk
1 egg

To serve

Whole cherries
Blue nasturtium (edible flower)

The terrine

To confit the duck legs, place them in a deep roasting tin, cover them in vegetable oil and bake in an oven at 120°C until the meat falls off the bone easily (this typically takes 1 ½ hrs). Set aside to cool. Finely dice the shallots and garlic, then sweat them off with the finely chopped thyme. Add the madeira and sherry to the garlic and shallots; reduce until all the liquid has evaporated.

Once it is cool, flake the confit duck meat and mix in the garlic and shallots; season to taste. Add the red wine jus, and mix well; using just enough so the duck all sticks together; put into your chosen moulds and set.

The cherry gel

Cook the cherries in a heavy-based pan with the star anise, clove, sugar and a small amount of water. Bring the mix to the boil and then add the agar agar. Leave to simmer for 5 mins. When the mix reaches boiling point the agar agar will activate. Remove the mix from the pan and transfer to a food processor. Blend until smooth and then place into a baking tray in the fridge to set. Once it has set, put it back into the food processor and add a small amount of water, blending until the mix has formed a loose gel. Set aside until needed.

The foie gras

Pass the foie gras through a fine sieve by pressing it through with a ladle or wooden spoon, and set aside in a bowl. Add the evaporated milk, cream, milk, shallots, peppercorns and bay leaf to a pan and slowly simmer for 5 mins. If using gelatine, soak it in cold water until it goes soft. Remove from the heat and take out the shallots, bay leaf and peppercorns. Slowly whisk the mixture into the foie gras (if using gelatine, add it) being careful not to add it too quickly, or the foie gras will split.

Once all the mixture is combined, return to the heat and slowly bring it to 70°C using a thermometer to ensure that the temperature is correct. Keep the mixture moving with a wooden spoon. Once the mousse reaches 70°C, remove from the heat and let cool, before passing it through a muslin cloth, and then pouring the mixture into an espuma gun. Give the espuma one charge of nitrous gas and leave in fridge for 4 hrs. If you are not using an espuma, place the mousse into a plastic container; leave in the fridge to set.

The gingerbread

Cream the butter and sugar together. Then add the mixed treacle and syrup, and keep blending until all the mix is combined. Slowly add the beaten egg, then all the dry ingredients. Finish by adding the milk, bit by bit. Pour into a standard loaf tin. Bake at 170°C for 45 mins. As soon as the gingerbread is cooked, remove from the oven and place on a rack to cool.

The whole cherries

Cut off the base and de-stone.

To serve

Remove the terrine from the moulds and place on a plate. Put a slice of gingerbread alongside the terrine. Prepare the espuma gun by shaking it and turning it upside down. Squirt the foie gras mousse on to the plate and arrange the cherries around it. Dot the cherry gel and add blue nasturtium leaves for garnish.

Pan fried scallops, asparagus, charred leeks & watercress purée

Serves: 6

Preparation time: 40 mins

For the scallops

12 hand-caught scallops
20ml vegetable oil
Unsalted butter

For the watercress purée

4 bunches of watercress
250ml fish stock
1 medium-sized onion
1 clove garlic
2 bay leaves
4 large sprigs of thyme
300ml double cream
50g unsalted butter

For the baby leeks & asparagus

1 bunch of baby leeks (about 8)
1 bunch of asparagus (about 12 asparagus spears)
50ml pomace oil
Salt and pepper

For the leek crisps

1 whole leek (white part only)

The scallops

To shuck the scallops, slide a large pallet knife along the flat side of the shell. Slowly ease the scallop from the shell, keeping the knife flat to the shell at all times. Once open, clean up the scallop, removing the gills, intestines and stomach. Depending on your preference keep or remove the roe. On this dish we have removed the roe. Once you have cleaned the scallops, leave them in the fridge.

When ready to cook, heat a pan until very hot; add a little oil. Add the scallops and cook for about 30 secs on each side, depending on how big they are, turning the scallops at least twice. Once you have turned them for the first time, add a little knob of butter to finish.

The watercress purée

Finely dice the onion and garlic. In a heavy-based pan, add the butter and sweat them down until translucent. Add the fish stock, bay leaves and thyme, and simmer until you have reduced the volume by half; now add the cream and reduce by half again. Pass the mix through a sieve and keep hot. Put the watercress into a blender and slowly add the cream reduction until you have a thick purée. Keep in the blender until smooth and then pass it through a fine sieve.

The baby leeks & asparagus

Bring a pan of seasoned water to the boil. Add the baby leeks and cook for about 3 mins. When cooked, add to iced water to cool down; the faster they cool, the more vibrant the colour will be. As soon as they are cold, remove from the water. Keep the water and repeat the process with the asparagus. To finish the asparagus, heat in boiling water; once it is hot, lightly coat it in pomace oil and season. To finish the baby leeks, coat them in pomace oil, char-grill until the grill lines appear on the side of the leeks. Season and serve.

The leek crisps

Lightly coat the leeks with olive oil and season with salt; deep fry at 150°C for 8 mins.

To serve

Place 2 dots of the purée c. 2cm in diameter in the centre with a gap between. Place the scallops either side.

Slice the asparagus spears in half; arrange alongside the scallops. Finish with leek crisps and a micro salad.

Slow roast cushion of veal, anchovies, tomato & parmesan

Serves: 6

Preparation time: 2½ hrs

For the slow roast veal

500g good quality veal cushion
Salt
White pepper

For the dressing

3 sprigs of parsley, chopped
1 clove garlic
8 black peppercorns, crushed
10g Dijon mustard
Sea salt
100g mayonnaise
10ml sherry vinegar
30ml water

To serve

Yellow tomato berries
1 banana shallot
8 caper berries
1 bunch mizuna
8 fillets silver skinned anchovies

The slow roast veal

Pre-heat the oven to 180°C. Trim the veal to ensure the meat is the same thickness throughout; this is important both for presentation and to ensure that it cooks evenly. Season the meat with salt and white pepper. Heat a frying pan until it is almost smoking, add a touch of vegetable oil and place the meat in the pan, sealing the outside evenly; this should take c.4 mins. Once it is golden all the way around, remove the veal from the pan and place it in a roasting tray. Roast the veal in the oven until the core temperature of the meat reaches 42°C. We recommend using a food-safe thermometer.

As soon as the veal has reached 42°C, it should be rested for around 8 mins; this allows the meat to relax and the natural juices to resurface. Once it has rested, the meat needs to be cooled as quickly as possible so it does not cook any further, so place it in the fridge and come back to it later.

Once it is cool, slice the veal as thinly as possible using a sharp knife with a thin, flat blade. Try not to push down on the veal as this will distort the shape of the meat and make it difficult to get even slices.

The dressing

Blend the parsley, parmesan, mustard, peppercorns and sherry vinegar in a blender, then blend until bright green. Add the mayonnaise and continue to blend until smooth. Finally add the water and season to taste with the sea salt. (Parmesan can be quite salty anyway, so you may not need to add much salt).

To serve

Cut the tomato berries and the caper berries in half. Arrange the slices of veal, tomatoes, anchovies and capers around one side of the plate leaving the other completely clean. Scatter some mizuna leaves on top. To finish drizzle with a touch of olive oil.

Heirloom tomatoes with Ragstone goat's cheese, watermelon & olives

Serves: 4

Preparation time: 30 mins (plus 90 mins for the watermelon)

For the tomatoes

200g heirloom tomatoes
½ bunch of basil
Olive oil
Salt and pepper
10ml red wine vinegar

For the watermelon

1 ripe watermelon

For the goat's cheese mousse

1 leaf gelatine
25ml full fat milk
50ml double cream
250g Ragstone goat's cheese
(though any other goat's cheese
will suffice, we prefer the flavour
of Ragstone)

For the olives

100g stoned olives

The tomatoes

Cut the tomatoes into a variety of different shapes. Arrange them on a plate and drizzle with a small amount of olive oil and vinegar. Add thinly-sliced basil leaves with salt and pepper to taste.

The watermelon

Peel the watermelon to reveal the bright red flesh. Cut this down into 4 quarters. (You only need a single quarter for this dish).

Cut the quarter you choose to use into a perfect square, and wrap it tightly in cling film. Place in a freezer for 1 ½ hrs. (At the Club we use a vacuum pack machine to create compressed watermelon, but in this case freezing will have a similar effect). After 1 ½ hrs, remove the watermelon from the freezer and cut into the desired shapes. At the Club, we normally slice it into rectangles that are about 1mm thick, but you can choose whatever shapes and sizes you like.

The goat's cheese mousse

Soak the gelatine in cold water in a small bowl. Remove and discard the outer rind of the goat's cheese. Crumble the cheese into the bowl of a food processor and blend until smooth. Gently heat the milk in a small pan and add the gelatine, making sure it dissolves. Slowly add the milk to the goat's cheese whilst the food processor is running. Once all the milk is fully combined with the cheese, add the double cream. Do not continue to blend for too long because the cream will split if it is worked too much. When ready, put the mix into a piping bag and put in the fridge to set.

To serve

Arrange the tomatoes, olives and watermelon on a plate and drizzle with olive oil and vinegar. Add thinly sliced basil leaves with salt and pepper to taste. At the Reform we would normally pipe the goat's cheese into a small glass pot and seal the lid. But you can pipe it directly onto the plate.

Wood pigeon with cheddar soil, mushroom salt, parsley root purée & chocolate pigeon jus

Serves: 10

Preparation time 1 hr 20 mins (10 mins cooking time)

For the pigeon

5 whole pigeons

For the mushroom salt

15 button mushrooms
3 tbsp white wine vinegar
Salt to taste

For the parsley crisps

30 leaves flat leaf parsley

For the cheddar soil

80g oats
16g popped popcorn
60g Bran Flakes breakfast cereal
150g cheddar cheese, finely grated
½ slice brown bread
6g olive oil
½ tbsp malt
3 tbsp water
50g butter

For the chocolate & pigeon jus

1 carrot
5 pigeon carcasses
4 shallots
2 cloves garlic
15 peppercorns
1 juniper berry
15 caraway seeds
Pinch of mustard seeds
20 button mushrooms
6 sprigs of thyme
300ml brandy
6 bay leaves
2 sticks celery
Dark chocolate to taste

For the parsley root purée

1kg parsley root (if not available, parsnip root can be substituted)
Double cream and an equal amount of whole milk
Salt to taste
100g butter

The pigeons

Remove breasts from pigeons and keep the carcasses for the sauce.

The mushroom salt

Grate the mushrooms very finely into a bowl and add the vinegar. Spread the mix out on a tray. Dehydrate at 52°C for around 2 hrs. Add salt to taste. If you do not have access to a dehydrator, leave in a very low oven (50°C to 70°C).

The parsley crisps

Cover a plate with clingfilm very tightly. Lightly brush the parsley leaves in olive oil and lay on the clingfilmed plate, and sprinkle the leaves with salt. Microwave the leaves for around 2 mins, checking regularly, until crispy. Then remove them from the plate and leave in a sealed container until needed.

The cheddar soil

Toast the oats gently under a grill. While the oats are toasting, put the butter into a hot pan and add a handful of popping corn; cover the pan and leave it until all corn is popped. Blend together the toasted oats and the popcorn in a food processor. Slowly add the Bran Flakes; once the ingredients start achieving a fine crumb consistency, slowly include the cheddar while blend constantly. Next add the brown bread. Finally, add the olive oil, malt and water, and season to taste. Leave in the fridge until needed.

The chocolate & pigeon jus

Roast the carcasses in an oven at about 180°C until crispy. Meanwhile, in a heavy-based pan with a little oil, sweat the carrot, shallots, garlic, and celery with a little oil over a low heat. Once the vegetables start to caramelise, add the brandy and flambé.(Stand away from the pan when doing so!) Once the flame is out, add the rest of the ingredients and the roasted bones. Cover the ingredients with water and reduce until the sauce is thick enough to coat the back of a spoon. Once reduced, pass through a sieve to remove the bits and then slightly reduce the mixture again over a high heat. Finally, add dark chocolate to taste (it is up to you how chocolately you would like it) and, if needed, add a small amount of sugar.

The parsley root purée

Peel and dice the parsley root. Cover it with a half-and-half mixture of milk and cream, and simmer till the parsley root is soft. Once cooked, remove the root from the liquid, and then blend it in a food processor with a small amount of the cream/milk mix. When the mix reaches a thick purée consistency, add the butter and adjust the seasoning to taste. Strain and chill until needed.

The pigeon breasts

Place the pigeon in a hot pan with a small amount of oil. Seal on both sides and then place in an oven at 190°C for 2 mins. Remove from the oven and rest for 2 mins before serving.

To serve

Place the cheddar crumb in a circular shape and put the carved pigeon breast on top. On the opposite side of the plate, spoon the parsley root purée into a circular shape of the same size. Sprinkle the mushroom salt on top of the purée and at 2 other points on the plate. Place the mushroom on top of one of the piles of salt and mirror this with a parsley leaf. Take a spoon full of the jus and using the very tip, spoon it onto the plate. Then, using the tip of the spoon drag the jus out to create a shape similar to a tear drop.

Guinea fowl terrine with crispy leg, baby gem lettuce purée & candied walnuts

Serves: 6

Preparation time: 4 hrs (allow 12 hrs to press the terrine)

For the guinea fowl legs

8 guinea fowl legs
2 sprigs thyme
4 cloves garlic
15 peppercorns
1 diced onion
Vegetable oil to cover
2 large chipping potatoes
200ml clarified butter

For the terrine

6 guinea fowl thighs and the meat of 2 legs
50g butter
2 medium shallots (finely diced)
1 clove garlic (finely diced)
20 tarragon leaves (finely diced)
200ml cooking wine
200ml chicken stock
30ml red wine jus

For the lettuce purée

1 medium onion
1 sprig thyme
25g unsalted butter
300ml chicken stock
150ml double cream
3 baby gem lettuces

For the candied walnuts

150g walnuts
500ml water
400g caster sugar
300ml vegetable oil

The guinea fowl

Pre-heat the oven to 120°C. Remove the thighs from the legs, slicing with a sharp knife around the top of the leg bone to remove any tendons. Season the legs and thighs with salt and pepper. Now heat a medium-sized pan with a little oil and seal the meat in a pan; once sealed, transfer the meat from the pan to a deep baking tray, and cover the meat with vegetable oil. Add the thyme, garlic, diced onion and peppercorns. Cover the tray with tin foil and place into the oven for about 1 hr 20 mins, until the meat is nearly falling off the bone.

Once the meat is cooked, remove the legs and thighs from the oil; leave them to cool. Once they are cool, pick the meat from all the thighs and two of the legs and set aside (for the terrine). Then with the remaining legs cut the knuckle off the leg bone with a quick single chopping action, clean any flesh or gristle off the bone and leave until needed later.

To finish the crispy legs: peel the potatoes, then on a mandolin turning slicer, turn the peeled potatoes until you are left with potato string. Coat the string in clarified butter. Pick two of the longest pieces of string you can find, and slowly begin to wrap them around the guinea fowl leg, from top to bottom. (This is quite tricky so might take a few attempts). Once complete, chill the wrapped legs slightly in the fridge. To finish, shallow fry both sides until crispy, then put into the oven until hot.

The terrine

Finely dice the shallots and garlic and chop the tarragon leaves. Heat a heavy-based saucepan with butter, add the shallots and garlic, and cook until transparent. Add the white wine to the pan and reduce until almost all of the wine has evaporated. Next, add the chicken stock to the pan, and again reduce it, this time until you are left with a thick-looking sauce at the bottom of the pan; now add your finely-chopped tarragon and the red wine jus.

Finally, add the flaked guinea fowl meat and mix well until all the ingredients are evenly combined. Put the guinea fowl mix into moulds and allow to set (overnight for a larger mould). Once the terrine has set, remove it from the moulds.

The lettuce purée

In a heavy-based saucepan, sauté the onion in the butter until translucent; then add the chicken stock and reduce it by half. Once the stock has reduced, add the cream and reduce by half again. Take the mix off the heat; pass it through a fine sieve and then season.

Slice the lettuce (keeping the hearts for garnish), blanch for 10 secs into boiling water and refresh straight after into ice water (the quicker this is done, the better colour you will have). Squeeze out any excess water through a muslin cloth. Now put the lettuce into a blender; slowly add the chicken stock/cream reduction as you blend. (You may not need all the reduction, so add it slowly until you have a very smooth consistency). Once smooth, pass it through a fine sieve and season to taste. Leave in the fridge until needed.

The candied walnuts

Blanch the walnuts by placing them in boiling water for c.30 secs, then removing them from the water and rubbing them in a tea towel; this will remove their skins. Next make a stock syrup by mixing the sugar and the water together. Bring the stock syrup to the boil and add the walnuts; leave them to simmer in the syrup for around 20 mins. Remove the walnuts and lay out on a tray to air dry and cool. Next, heat a pan with the vegetable oil. Heat the oil gently, and then shallow fry the walnuts until they are crispy.

To serve

Place the lettuce purée into two heaps slightly apart. Then, using the tip of your spoon drag the purée into two 'swipes' parallel to each other. Place the terrine across the purée at an angle and stand the hot leg against it. Crush some candied walnuts and scatter them around the plate. Then arrange the lettuce hearts as garnish.

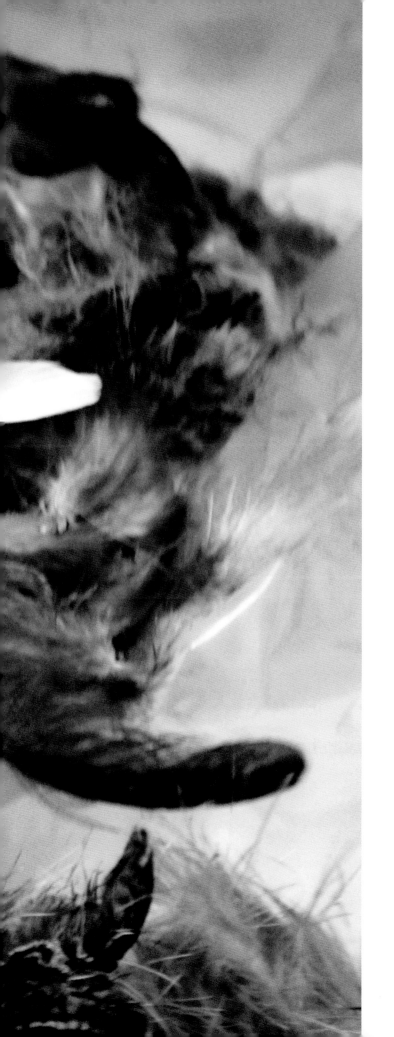

FOOD PREPARATION

Fish preparation

A round fish can be the hardest type to fillet. Fish such as sea bass, sea bream, mackerel and cod are of this type.

Start by checking the fish for signs of freshness. The smell will be the first thing, as fresh fish should smell like the ocean. If it smells really fishy then it is not fresh. Then check the gills; when a fish is fresh the gills are bright red and full of blood. The darker the gills are, the longer the fish has been out of the water. The eyes of the fish should be bright and glossy with the flesh being firm yet bouncy. Once you are happy with the quality of your fish, it is time to fillet it.

The filleting process that we are describing is a standard for all round fish. The images use a mackerel to illustrate this. Start with placing the fish onto a chopping board. If you can put a non-slip mat or tea towel under the board, this should prevent it from slipping. Hold the fish belly up: a small hole should be visible around the middle of your fish. Using a sharp filleting knife, slice upwards from the hole to the head and remove the guts. Give the fish a quick rinse under the cold tap to remove any excess blood and dry with a cloth. Place back on the chopping board with the head pointing away from you. Make two incisions that run from the gills to the head with straight sweeping motions.

Using the tip of the knife slice the fish from the head to tail in one smooth movement. Keeping the knife flush to the bone, repeat the slicing action until the fillet comes away from the frame. Repeat this process for the other side.

You should be left with two clean, smooth fillets. Next, you will need a pair of tweezers to remove the pin bones that run down the centre of the fillet. To remove just pull them gently with the tweezers, removing the bones one by one. Another way to do this is to cut the bones out, but do this carefully or you could cut the fillet in half by mistake. When all bones are removed trim away the fat on the belly side of the fillet. The fish is now ready to cook.

Rabbit preparation

Place the rabbit on a chopping board. This can be quite a messy job, so you may wish to put down some newspaper around the chopping board. Start by using a small knife. Make an incision in the skin on the knee of the rabbit's hind legs. Push the knee from underneath, forcing it through the skin. It should just pop out to fully expose the leg. Then repeat with the other leg. Now you should be left with two exposed legs and a lump of excess skin still attached to the rabbit's forelegs. Grasp the excess skin and, holding the rabbit's legs firmly in one hand, pull the skin over the top of the rabbit. It will come off in one piece and can now be discarded. Now you are left with a whole rabbit, ready to prepare. Remove the head with a large knife or cleaver. Make an incision down the stomach and remove the internal organs. These can either be discarded or they can be used to make such things as pâtés. Wash the rabbit and dry well with a kitchen cloth. Keep refrigerated until you are ready to use it.

Bird preparation

Stand a carrier bag in a sink, ensuring the sides of the bag are up. This will catch any falling feathers. Lay down some newspaper in the surrounding area; this will make cleaning up much easier.

Hold the bird by its back, so it is facing you. Gently brush the feathers upwards so that they stand away from the bird. With small, gentle movements, start plucking the feathers into the carrier bag. If you notice any skin coming away with the feathers you are being too rough. Experiment a little with this until you find the most efficient method for you. When the front of the bird is featherless, turn the bird over and repeat for its back.

Once the back and front are finished, spread the tail feathers and pluck these following the line of the feathers. Next, remove the leg feathers. Lay the bird on its back and pluck the feathers away from you using a sharp action. The trick to this is a short and precise plucking movement.

Gutting the bird

Using a sharp knife, remove the head, feet and wings. Cut off the tail end of the bird and remove the internal organs through the hole. Rinse the inside to remove any excess blood. Refrigerate the bird for a couple of days before using.

MAINS

Roast fillet of pork, crispy pigs' ears, leek with oregano & lemon potatoes

Serves: 8

Preparation time: 48 hrs (for the brining and cooking of the pigs' ears) or 3 hrs (without the pigs' ears)

For the ears

2 pigs' ears
1 carrot
1 onion (chopped)

For the pork tenderloin

4 pork tenderloins
Zest of 2 lemons
¼ of a bunch of oregano (finely chopped)
Black pepper
Olive oil

For the pulled pork

2kg pork shoulder or belly pork
2 onions (sliced)
6 cloves garlic (sliced)
8 caraway seeds

1 tbsp paprika
¼ of a bunch of oregano (rough chopped)
1 tbsp whole grain mustard
Salt and pepper
180ml white wine vinegar
260ml cider

For the brine

1kg salt
½ litre water
5 peppercorns
2 bay leaves
Sprig of thyme
10 coriander seeds
5 fennel seeds

For the paprika salt

2 tbsp dark brown sugar
4 tbsp salt
1 tbsp garlic powder
½ tbsp paprika

For the leek pieces

2 leeks

For the leek purée

2 leek whites
3 shallots
2 garlic cloves
3 sprigs of thyme
2 leek greens
150ml chicken stock

For the oregano and lemon potatoes

8 large potatoes
Juice of 2 lemons
150g melted butter
¼ bunch of oregano
40ml olive oil
1 tbsp Dijon mustard
1 bay leaf
2 shallots
1 clove garlic
2 sprigs of thyme

To serve

Nasturtium leaves

Previous page: Roast fillet of pork, crispy pigs' ears, leek with oregano & lemon potatoes

The crispy pigs' ears

Place all the brine ingredients into a pan, and slowly heat until all salt has dissolved. Then remove the pan from the heat and let it cool. Once the water is cool, place the pigs' ears in the brine and leave for 24 hrs. Remove the ears from the brine and wash them in fresh water. Next put the ears into a pan with a carrot, chopped onion and with water to cover.

Simmer gently for 3 hrs 15 mins. Then lay baking parchment onto a flat tray and place the ears on the parchment. Now place another sheet of baking parchment on top of the ears, and another flat tray on top of that; press until the ears are flat, and then put a weight on them and leave until cool. Then slice the ears in 6mm thin strips. For the paprika salt combine all the ingredients in a small mixing bowl. To finish deep fry the strips and dust with paprika salt.

The pork tenderloin

Start by removing any sinew from the pork tenderloin. Cut the tenderloins in half to give you 8 portions. Set aside. Cut the baking paper into small rectangles long enough that it is able to wrap 1½ times around your individual tenderloin portions. Once the paper is measured lay all 8 pieces of parchment out on a work surface and put a good splash of olive oil on each one.

Next sprinkle the oregano, lemon zest and black pepper across each sheet. Then lay each tenderloin on a piece of paper. Roll the meat over the herbs and oil, wrapping the paper completely around each of the tenderloins. Once all are rolled in the paper, roll each tenderloin in aluminium foil and twist the ends. When ready to cook preheat oven to 190˚C. Place your tenderloin parcels on a tray and bake for 11-14 mins.

The pulled pork

Pre-heat your oven to 165˚C. Place the pork on a tray and rub in oil. Now cover the pork with the cider and vinegar and the garlic and onions. Mix together the paprika, mustard, caraway seeds and chopped oregano. Completely coat the pork with this mix. Season with salt and pepper. Cover the meat with parchment paper and then aluminium foil. Place the pork in the oven and roast for 3-4 hrs or until it can be pulled with a fork. Remove from oven and shred. Set aside and let cool. To reheat warm up with a little of the pork jus, a knob of butter and season to taste.

The leek pieces

Place a pan of seasoned water on your stove and bring to boil. Meanwhile, cut a leek into 10cm pieces. When you start to get to the really dark green part of the leek stop, as this can be quite bitter. Cut the pieces in half length ways and remove the layers. Once you have the individual layers of the leek, blanch them in the boiling water. This will only take a matter of seconds. Once cooked, remove from the pan and refresh in cold icy water. Once cold, remove from the water and set aside until needed.

The leek purée

Finely dice the shallots, garlic and leek whites. Sweat the vegetables off in a heavy-based pan with a little butter and oil and thyme sprigs. Add chicken stock and reduce slightly. Wash the leek greens then blanch in boiling water, remove from the water and refresh in icy cold water. Add the leek and chicken stock mix to a food processor and blend. Add the blanched leek greens. This will help improve the colour of your purée. As soon as it is smooth, remove from food processor and pass through a fine sieve. Chill as soon as possible to maintain the colour of the purée. Set aside.

The oregano and lemon potatoes

Peel and cut the potatoes into the shape you want. Heat the olive oil in a pan. Add the potatoes. Add the diced shallot, garlic, thyme, bay, oregano, Dijon mustard and butter. Season the potatoes with salt and pepper. Cover the potatoes with chicken stock (you could use water instead of stock), place into a pre-heated oven at 170˚C for 35-45 mins.

To serve

Slice the pork tenderloin into three, place in a diagonal line across the plate. Place two potatoes on opposite sides on the pork. Put dots of the leek purée around the plate and arrange the leek pieces. Top with the crispy pigs' ears, the hot pulled pork and nasturtium leaves.

Gnocchi with mushroom velouté, sautéed wild mushrooms & grilled potatoes

Serves: 6

Preparation time: 2 ½ hrs

For the gnocchi

1kg desirée potatoes (or other waxy potato)
400g pasta flour
100g parmesan
3 eggs
30g salt

For the mushroom velouté

75g unsalted butter
2 shallots, diced
250g button mushrooms, sliced
175ml vegetable stock
300ml double cream

For the grilled potatoes

6 large new potatoes
Salt and pepper
25ml of olive oil

For the green leek diamonds

Green of 1 leek

For the wild mushrooms

300g wild mushrooms
10g clarified butter

To serve

Red mustard frilles (microherb)
Raw mushrooms

The gnocchi

Pre-heat the oven to 180°C. Place the potatoes on a baking tray with a layer of salt underneath, and bake in the oven; cooking times will vary depending on the size of the potato (you can test with a skewer). Once the potatoes are cooked, scoop out the insides and pass the flesh through a fine sieve; this will leave you with c.600g of potato for the gnocchi mix. Mix in all the ingredients and form a dough; if your dough is looking a little wet, knead in a little more flour. Roll the dough out to a thin sausage and cut it into pieces 2 ½ cm long. Cook the gnocchi in seasoned boiling water for 2 mins.

The mushroom velouté

Melt the butter in a pan and sweat off the diced shallots until they are translucent. Add the mushrooms and cook until all liquid has evaporated. Add the vegetable stock and cream, and then simmer for about 15 mins over a low heat. Blend in a food processor until smooth. Pass through a fine sieve and serve when required.

The grilled potatoes

Boil the potatoes in a pan of seasoned water until they are only just cooked. Refresh them in iced water, peel and slice into 1 cm thick pieces. Marinade in olive oil until needed. To serve grill both sides.

The green leek diamonds

Take the dark green part of the leek, flatten it onto a chopping board and slice lengthways down the middle. Diagonally cut 3cm strips parallel to each other; you will end up with a diamond effect. Blanch the leek diamonds in seasoned boiling water, when required.

The sautéed wild mushrooms

Get a pan hot on the stove, with a little bit of clarified butter in it. Put in the wild mushroom and sauté. Check the seasoning and serve.

To serve

Arrange the gnocchi, sautéed wild mushrooms, leek diamonds and potatoes on top of the velouté. Then garnish with red mustard frilles and sliced raw mushroom.

Pan fried sea bass with confît fennel, tomatoes, tapenade & wine-infused potatoes

Serves: 4

Preparation time: 50 mins

For the bass

4 fillets of sea bass

For the confît fennel

4 bulbs baby fennel
500ml vegetable oil

For the olive tapenade

1 medium clove garlic
2 tbsp capers
100g black olives
2 tbsp fresh parsley
1 tbsp fresh lemon juice
2 tbsp extra virgin olive oil
Salt
Black pepper

For the tomatoes

200g heritage tomatoes

For the infused wine

500ml white wine
2 shallots, diced
4 basil stalks
1 clove garlic, crushed

For the potatoes

2 large baking potatoes
50g ice cold butter, diced
Salt and pepper

The confît fennel

Trim the baby fennel and place in a pan with vegetable oil. Put the pan on the *lowest* heat possible; if the oil gets too hot not only will the fennel burn but it could spit. Leave until the fennel is soft; this should take c. 20 mins. Remove from the oil and leave to cool.

The tapenade and tomatoes

Combine all the ingredients and pulse until a paste is formed (we keep it fairly coarse). Season to taste. Slice tomatoes: we recommend heritage tomatoes for their variety of size, shape and colour.

The infused wine

Dice and sweat the shallots and garlic until they are translucent, add the wine and basil stalks. Bring the liquid up to a boil and leave to simmer on a low heat till the flavours have infused (c. 20 mins). You will add this to the potatoes later.

The potatoes

Cut the baking potatoes into slices c.1cm thick, and then cut out the desired shape using a cutter (we normally use rounds). Half cook the potatoes in seasoned water, transfer them to a hot pan and fry them in a little butter until they are golden on both sides. Add the confît fennel, some basil leaves and the infused wine, and bring the mixture to just below boiling. When everything is hot, emulsify in the butter cubes one at a time, keeping the pan moving until the sauce thickens.

The sea bass

Pan fry the fish in butter over a medium heat, skin side down; add a little more butter when turning the fish. Finish in the oven for 3 mins at 180°C.

To serve

Arrange tomatoes in the bottom of a bowl. Stack the fennel, potatoes and whole olives on top of the tomato. Lay the fish on top of the fennel, skin facing up and top with the olive tapenade. Drizzle the sauce from the potatoes around the plate.

Roast Hardwick salt-marsh lamb with mint, broad beans, tomato & new potatoes

Serves: 6

Preparation time: 4 hrs

For the broth
7 egg whites
500g lean lamb mince
2 litres lamb stock
2 tbsp tomato purée
1 bay leaf
8 sprigs of thyme
4 black peppercorns
1 carrot, finely diced
1 stick celery, finely diced
1 onion, finely diced

For the lamb
6 lamb rumps each of 230g; we prefer salt-marsh lamb for this dish

To finish
200g frozen broad beans
4 plum tomatoes
Mint leaves, finely shredded

The broth

Brown the lamb mince in a deep pot. When brown, strain through a colander to remove any excess fat and put back into the pot. Add the diced vegetables, peppercorns and bay leaf, and cook for a further 10 mins. Add the lamb stock and whisk in the egg whites. Turn the heat up to high and leave until the egg begins to coagulate; this will make the egg float to the top, bringing with it any fats or impurities. This will look like dirty foam floating on top of the broth; do not worry – this is what is supposed to happen! Once the egg whites and impurities have risen to the surface, turn down the heat and leave the pan to simmer for a further 45 mins. Do not let it boil as this will cause the foam to break up and make the broth cloudy. After 45 mins, pass the broth through a fine sieve, being careful not to mix the foam in with the broth. You should be left with a clear liquid.

The lamb

Pre-heat the oven to 180°C. Place a heavy pan on a high heat until almost smoking; seal the outside of the rump, before placing in the oven. We serve lamb medium rare at the Club. To do this cook the lamb for around 8 mins.

To finish

Soak the broad beans in cold water till defrosted. Then deshell them and place to one side. Deseed and dice the plum tomatoes and finely shred the mint leaves.

To serve

Arrange the broad beans and tomatoes into the centre of a deep plate. Cut the ends from the lamb rump and carve into three, ensuring that you cut across the grain. Place lamb on the top of the garnish. You can finish by ripping a few mint leaves into the broth.

Hake with pear, beetroot, goat's cheese mousse & peanuts

Serves: 6

Preparation time: 1 hr 20 mins

For the diced beetroot

1 large raw beetroot
50ml red wine vinegar
800ml water
20 yellow mustard seeds
1 sprig of thyme
Salt and pepper
30g caster sugar
2 cloves garlic

For the beetroot & apple purée

2 large raw beetroots
1 apple
1 clove garlic
2 sprigs of thyme
25g unsalted butter
18g caster sugar
75ml water

For the goat's cheese mousse

250g goat's cheese log
25ml full fat milk
1 gelatine leaf
50ml double cream

For the peanut mix

300g peanuts
250ml honey
400ml water
350g caster sugar
45g poppy seeds

For the hake

6 portions of hake

For the pear

2 pears

To serve

Curly lettuce

The diced beetroot

Dice the beetroot into uniform cubes, keeping the trimmings on one side. Place the diced beetroot in a pan with the vinegar, water, thyme, sugar, garlic, mustard seeds and seasoning. Bring to a simmer and leave until the beetroot is cooked. When cooked remove from the pan and set aside.

The beetroot & apple purée

Dice the beetroot and start to cook out in a pan on a low heat with the butter. When the beetroot is half cooked (when the beetroot is half cooked a knife will only slide part way in) add the apple, garlic, thyme, water and sugar, and continue to cook. Once cooked, remove the mixture from the pan and put into a food processor; blend until smooth and season to taste. Pass through a fine sieve and put to one side for later use.

The goat's cheese mousse

Soak the gelatine in cold water. Roughly crumble the goat's cheese and place it in a food processor, and blend until smooth. Warm the milk in a small bowl and add the softened gelatine to dissolve. Add the milk/gelatine mix to the goat's cheese and blend until an even smooth texture. To avoid splitting, slowly add the double cream and blend until fully combined, then put into a piping bag and leave in the fridge until needed.

The peanut mix

Bring the honey, water and sugar to the boil over a medium heat and add the peanuts; turn the heat down and simmer for 30 mins. Remove the nuts from the liquid and leave on kitchen roll to dry. Heat a pan with enough oil and shallow fry the nuts. When they are cooked, remove the peanuts

from the oil and leave them to cool. Break the nuts using a rolling pin, keeping some whole. Mix the poppy seeds in with the peanuts.

The hake

Rub a little olive oil onto the hake and season with salt and pepper. Lay the hake skin side down in a hot pan. Press down slightly on the flesh of the fish to ensure the skin has full contact with the pan. Once the skin has a nice even golden colour, remove it from the pan and place in an oven at 180°C for c.4 mins or until the fish is cooked.

The sliced pear

Cut the pears into halves and remove the seeds. Slice into pieces length ways. It is best to leave this until just before serving to avoid the pear oxidising.

To serve

Using a dessert spoon, tip the beetroot purée onto the plate whilst using a swiping action to create two straight lines down the centre. Place the hake on top of the purée. Pipe the goat's cheese at random intervals around the plate and arrange the diced beetroot and pears. Sprinkle liberally with the peanut mix.

Ox cheek ravioli with Roscoff onions, kale, baby parsnips, onion crumb & parsnip cream

Serves: 6

Preparation time: 6 hrs (including 3 hrs cooking for the ox cheek)

For the pasta

See pasta recipe p.115

For the braised ox cheek filling

800g ox cheek
300ml red wine
1 carrot, diced
1 stick celery, diced
½ leek, diced
1 onion, diced
1 litre veal stock (see p.106)

1 tbsp tomato purée
1 beaten egg

For the Roscoff onions

4 Roscoff (pink) onions
Olive oil
Salt and pepper

For the parsnip cream

2 parsnips
200ml whole milk
1 onion
1 sprig of thyme
2 bay leaves
1 clove garlic
25g unsalted butter

For the kale

300g kale

For the onion crumb

1 onion
50g corn flour
Salt and pepper

For the baby parsnips

6 baby parsnips

The braised ox cheek filling

Season the ox cheek and brown in a hot pot. Add the vegetables and caramelise. Add the tomato purée and cook until the moisture has gone. Pour in the red wine to deglaze the pan and continue to cook until the alcohol has evaporated. Then add the veal stock, cover, and cook slowly until the ox cheek falls apart; this should take c. 3 hrs. When cooked, remove the ox cheek from the sauce and shred into small pieces. Leave to cool. Blend until smooth. Sieve, then stir the ox cheek meat back into the sauce.

The ravioli

Flour your worktop. Roll the pasta until it is 1mm thick (grade 1 if you are using a pasta machine). Spread the pasta sheet out on the work top. Place a tsp of the ox cheek filling at regular intervals along one side of the pasta. Use the beaten egg to wash around the mixture and fold the pasta sheet in half to cover the ox filling. Press down around the filling to ensure that there is no air inside. Cut the pasta into the desired shape. Cook the ravioli in salted, boiling water. Once the pasta is cooked and the inside is piping hot, serve.

The Roscoff onions

Peel the onions, keeping them whole. Cut in half through the root, making sure the root remains attached. In a hot pan with a splash of oil, colour the onions until very dark. Then place in a baking tray with olive oil, salt and pepper. Roast in the oven at 180°C for 20 mins. Remove the root; spilt the layers of the onion and serve hot.

The parsnip cream

Dice the onion and crush the garlic. Dice the parsnips. Sweat the onion and garlic until they are translucent. Add the parsnips to the onion and garlic along with the milk, thyme, bay leaves and butter. When cooked remove the bay leaves and blend until smooth. Season to taste and pass through a fine sieve.

The kale and baby parsnips

Cook in boiling, salted water.

The onion crumb

Thinly slice the onion on a mandolin and coat with the corn flour. Shallow fry in a pan of oil until crisp. Dry the onions to remove any excess oil; then blend and leave to cool.

To serve

Smear the parsnip purée onto one side of the plate and top with the onion crumb and kale. Arrange the ravioli on the opposite side to the parsnip. Lean the Roscoff onion and baby parsnips against the ravioli.

Lamb Cutlets Reform

Serves: 4

Preparation time: 45 mins

For the lamb cutlets

8 lamb cutlets, French-trimmed
75g ham
50g cooked ox tongue
50g cooked beetroot
25g gherkins
2 eggs
50g breadcrumbs

For the Reform jus

150ml lamb stock
1 tsp tomato purée
35ml tarragon vinegar (white wine vinegar is fine)
50ml red wine
2 tbsp redcurrant jelly
2 peppercorns
1 shallot
2 cloves garlic
35g unsalted butter

Developed by Alexis Soyer himself, in response to a member demanding 'something different' after the kitchens had closed. It has never left the Club menu since.

The lamb cutlets

Separate the egg yolks from the whites. Place the egg whites in cling film and steam over boiling water until firm; then remove them from the heat and chill. Beat the egg yolks. Season the lamb cutlets with salt and pepper, then coat them with flour and dip into the beaten yolks. Now cover the lamb cutlets in an even layer of breadcrumbs. Place in a frying pan with butter and gently cook on a medium heat for approximately 2 mins each side until golden. Then place in an oven for 6 mins at 180°C.

The Reform jus

Finely chop the shallots and garlic. Melt the butter in a pan over a moderate heat; add the shallots and garlic and cook for approximately one minute. Add the tomato purée and stir for a further minute; then add the vinegar, red wine and peppercorns and reduce by a third of the volume. Add the stock and redcurrant jelly and again reduce, this time by a half. Finally, add the batons of ham, beetroot, ox tongue, gherkins and egg white.

To serve

Place the Reform jus into the bottom of a bowl. Arrange the batons in a pile in the middle of the bowl. Place the lamb cutlets into the bowl so they lean on the batons.

Breaded lamb breast with sweetbreads, squash & braised salsify

Serves: 6

Preparation time: 24 hrs
(to allow lamb breast to press overnight)

For the lamb breast

1 whole lamb breast
1 litre vegetable oil
1 bulb garlic
1 onion
5 large sprigs of rosemary
7 coriander seeds

For the pané

50g bread crumbs
2 eggs
50g flour
100ml milk

For the Parisian scoops of squash

1 whole squash

For the squash purée

Squash trimmings
100g butter
½ tsp ground cinnamon
¼ tsp ground nutmeg
2 tbsp dark brown sugar
100ml double cream
Salt and pepper to taste

For the braised salsify

250g salsify
70ml sherry

2 shallots, sliced
2 cloves garlic, crushed
5 sprigs of rosemary
100g unsalted butter
200ml red wine jus
Juice of 1 lemon

For the sweetbreads

400g sweetbreads
Salt and pepper

The lamb and pané

Place the lamb into a deep casserole pot or deep baking tray, and fill the tray with the oil, onion, garlic, coriander seeds and rosemary. Cook in the oven at 120°C for 2-3 hrs, or until the bones can be removed with ease. When removing the tray from the oven, be careful of the hot oil. Remove the lamb breast from the oil and take out the bones.

Press the lamb breast between two trays and wrap tightly in cling film. Place a weight on top of the trays and chill in the fridge. Once chilled, remove the lamb from between the trays and cut into strips, 1cm wide and 6cm in length; you will need two per portion. Beat the eggs and milk, cover the lamb strips in flour and dip in the beaten egg; then coat them in breadcrumbs. When ready to serve, shallow fry them until the breadcrumbs turn golden, check that the middle is hot, and serve immediately.

The Parisian scoops of squash

Using a large Parisian scoop or a small melon baller, remove balls from the whole squash. Cook these slowly in seasoned water.

The squash purée

Remove the skin from the squash and finely slice the flesh. Add the butter, cinnamon, nutmeg and sugar to a pan over a medium heat, and cook for 3 mins; then add the squash and sweat it. Once the squash is cooked, add the cream and bring to the boil. Then put the mixture into a food processor

and blend until smooth. Season the purée to taste and pass through a fine sieve.

The braised salsify

Peel the salsify under running water. When peeled put into water and lemon juice to avoid the salsify oxidizing. Cut the salsify into three inch batons and return to the lemon water. Sweat the shallots and garlic with 5g of the butter in a pan over a medium heat. Once the shallots are translucent, add the salsify and sweat for a further 2 mins; then add the sherry and the rosemary and cook until the alcohol has evaporated. Once the sherry has cooked out, add the red wine jus and the remaining butter. Cover the pan with parchment paper and cook until the salsify is soft.

The sweetbreads

Peel the outer membrane off the sweetbreads. Put a pan on a high heat and leave until almost smoking. Season the sweetbreads with salt and pepper. Put a small amount of oil in the pan, followed by the sweetbreads. Pan fry until golden on both sides. Serve immediately.

To serve

Start by arranging the lamb breast, sweetbreads and salsify randomly around the base of the plate. Dot the squash purée into the gaps and finish with the Parisian scoops and a drizzle of the jus.

Poached cod cheeks with Puy lentils, leeks & cucumber

Serves: 8

Preparation time: 3 hrs

For the cod cheeks

2kg cod cheeks
200ml milk
500ml fish stock
150g butter
2 bay leaves
1 sprig of thyme
15 fennel seeds
1 onion
15 coriander seeds
10 peppercorns

For the Puy lentils

500g Puy lentils
3 shallots, finely diced
4 sticks celery, finely diced
½ red chilli
2 bay leaves
1 litre fish stock (to cover)
Bouquet garni

For the leek purée

2 leeks (separated into white & green parts)
3 shallots
2 garlic cloves
3 sprigs of thyme
150ml chicken stock

For the leek round

White part of 1 leek

For the lozenge cucumber

1 cucumber

To serve

Blue nasturtium or other edible flowers

The Puy lentils

Wash the lentils under cold running water. In a pan, melt the butter and add the vegetables, sweating them until they appear translucent. Add the Puy lentils, bay and bouquet garni, cover with fish stock and simmer over a low heat until the lentils are cooked. Season to taste.

The leek purée

Finely dice the shallots, garlic and leek whites, then sweat them off in a heavy-based pan with a little butter, oil, and the thyme. Add the chicken stock and reduce slightly.

Wash the leek greens, blanch in boiling water; immediately refresh in icy cold water (to preserve the vibrant green colour). Blend the leek and chicken stock mix, and add the leek greens to improve the colour of your purée. When smooth, pass through a fine sieve; chill as soon as possible.

The leek round

Slice the leek at 1½ cm intervals so you are left with circles of leek. Blanch in seasoned boiling water and immediately refresh in cold icy water. Set aside; when needed again warm them in boiling water.

The lozenge cucumber

Cut the cucumber in half lengthways and remove any seeds. Cut diagonally at 3cm intervals along the cucumber, keeping the cuts parallel to each other – you end up with a diamond effect.

The cod cheeks

Place the cod cheeks in a shallow pan, cover with all of the ingredients and simmer gently. They will take c.3-4 mins to cook. We recommend you do this when you are ready to serve them.

To serve see opposite page

To serve

Spoon the leek purée along the bottom of the bowl and place the lentils on top ensuring you spoon in a good amount of the cooking liquid. Arrange the poached cod cheeks, leek rounds, lozenge cucumber on the top of the lentils. We suggest blue nasturtium or other edible flowers as garnish.

Roast loin of rabbit with black pudding purée, baby carrots & savoy cabbage

Serves: 4

Preparation time: 3 hrs

For the rabbit loins

2 rabbit saddles
50g lamb caul fat
2 sprigs of sage

For the rabbit balls

4 rabbit legs
Vegetable oil
1 small savoy cabbage
4 sprigs of sage
3 sprigs of thyme
6 cloves garlic

For the black pudding purée

100g black pudding

For the carrot purée

2 good sized carrots
2 shallots
100ml double cream
50g unsalted butter

For the baby carrots

8 baby carrots
Salt and pepper

For the bacon foam

100g good quality bacon
500ml milk
500ml cream
2 sprigs of thyme
100g unsalted butter

To serve

Carrot tops

The rabbit balls wrapped in savoy cabbage

Place the rabbit legs into a deep saucepan with the garlic and half the thyme. Cover the meat with the vegetable oil. Cook on a low heat for c.40 mins until the meat starts to fall away from the bone. Remove the meat from the pan and strain. Pick the flesh from the bones and put in a bowl with a small amount of the oil. Roll the meat into golf ball-sized portions and set aside.

Peel the four outer leaves from the savoy cabbage and lay them flat on a chopping board. With a sharp knife, remove the core of the leaves. Blanch the leaves in seasoned, boiling water and, when just cooked, put immediately into iced water; this will keep the colour as vibrant as possible.

Lay out a sheet of cling film and remove any creases by rubbing it. Repeat this process twice, placing each sheet on top of the other (so that you end up with 3 layers of cling film). Lay the cabbage leaves out on the cling film and place the balls of rabbit in the centre of the leaves. Wrap the cabbage tightly around the rabbit and wrap the layered cling film around the balls. Twist the cling film to ensure there is no air left inside, and secure by tying string around the knot. When you are ready to serve them, place in boiling water for 8 mins.

The baby carrots

Bring a pan of water to boil; add the baby carrots and leave to boil for c.5mins. Quickly rub off the outer skin of the carrots and serve.

The black pudding purée

Break the black pudding into small pieces, pulse in a food processor until smooth. Place into a piping bag. Set aside.

The rabbit loins

Wash the caul fat in cold water for c.5 mins. Cut the fat into 2 pieces that are large enough to wrap the loins completely and lay out on cling film. Remove the loins from the rabbit saddle and place with two sage leaves on the caul fat, leaving a 1 cm gap between each. Pipe the black pudding purée in between the loins, keeping it as uniform as possible. Season the loins with salt and pepper. Carefully pick up one side of the cling film and fold the caul fat over the rabbit (ensuring not to wrap the cling film in with the rabbit) and roll into a ballotine. Push the air out of either side, twist the ends of the cling film and tie the ends using string. When done, the cling film should feel bouncy to touch and completely tight; if there is any air inside it will not work. Place the rabbit in the fridge to set the black pudding. When all the other elements are done it will be time to cook the rabbit. Heat a frying pan with a drop of vegetable oil and pan fry the rabbit until evenly golden brown. When you are happy with the colour, place in an oven proof roasting dish and cook at c.180°C for 8 mins, then rest in a warm place for c.10 mins.

The carrot purée

Peel and dice the carrots and shallots into 1 cm squares. Place a pan on a medium heat with a dash of vegetable oil. Add the shallots with the caraway seeds and sweat off. Add the carrots and cook for a further 10 mins. Add 100ml of double cream and a generous knob of butter. Reduce by half and season. Blend until completely smooth (if the purée looks too dry you can add a touch more cream). Pass through a fine sieve and keep hot.

The bacon foam

Dice the bacon and place in a saucepan. Brown the bacon until golden and crisp. Add the milk, cream and a couple of sprigs of thyme, ensuring that your pan is not too hot as the cream will burn. Leave to infuse for c.10 mins and pass this through a fine sieve. When serving, use a small hand blender to emulsify the butter into the hot liquid and blend until the liquid begins to froth. Tilt the pan slightly to collect the foam from the corner of the pan using a table spoon. Serve immediately.

To serve

Slice each rabbit loin into 6 slices, discarding the very ends. Smear the carrot purée using a dessert spoon to form a tear drop effect. Arrange the rabbit on top of the purée and place the rabbit ball at one end. Place the baby carrots and carrot tops around the rabbit. Spoon on the bacon foam and serve immediately.

Previous page: Roast loin of rabbit with black pudding purée, baby carrots & savoy cabbage

Sea trout with sea vegetables & lemon butter sauce

Serves: 4

Preparation time: 30 mins

For the trout

4 portions (160g each) of wild
sea trout.(scaled and pin boned)
Vegetable oil
Salt and pepper
Unsalted butter

For the sea vegetables

100g samphire
100g sea purslane (fine beans
can be used as a substitute)
100g sea aster (spinach can be
used as a substitute)

For the lemon butter sauce

Zest and juice of 1 large lemon
100ml white wine
25ml double cream
2 white peppercorns
1 banana shallot
5 fennel seeds
250g cold butter, diced

The trout

Heat a non-stick pan, with a touch of vegetable oil, on a high heat. Season the fish with salt and pepper and place in the pan, skin side down, laying it away from you to avoid any oil splashing. Press down on the flesh slightly to ensure all the skin is in contact with the pan; this will ensure all of the skin goes crispy. Add a generous knob of butter and turn the fish. Continue to cook until the trout reaches your preference; we serve trout slightly pink but it is down to personal taste.

The sea vegetables

Wash all the sea vegetables thoroughly to remove any excess salt. Heat a pan on the stove with a small amount of butter and toss in the sea vegetables. Cook until tender, though still with a slight bite. Season to taste.

The lemon butter sauce

Sweat off the shallots in a pan over a medium heat until they are translucent; then add the peppercorns and fennel seeds. Deglaze the pan with the white wine and continue to cook until the alcohol has evaporated then add the double cream. Whisk in the cold butter piece by piece. Do not add the butter too fast or the sauce will split. When all the butter is emulsified, add the lemon juice and zest. Strain the liquid through a fine sieve. Serve the sauce warm.

To serve

Spoon the sea vegetables onto the plate, creating a pile in the centre. Spoon the lemon butter sauce into the centre creating an even surface under the vegetables; 3-4 dessert spoons should be sufficient. Place the trout fillet, skin side up, on top of the vegetables.

Red onion tarte tatin, goat's cheese, shallot purée & rocket

Serves: 6

Preparation time: 3 hrs

For the red onion tarte tatin
150g soft light brown sugar
100ml water
35ml double cream
50g cold diced butter
3 whole sprigs of rosemary
3 large red onions
Olive oil
Salt and pepper
Beaten egg for wash
1 pack ready rolled puff pastry
(we hand make our puff pastry
at the Club but for ease we
suggest using ready rolled)

For the shallot purée
50g unsalted butter
8 shallots, finely diced
1 clove of garlic, finely diced
1 sprig of thyme, chopped
½ milk and ½ double cream
(enough to cover)
Salt and pepper

For the baby onions
30 baby silver skin onions
Butter
Vegetable oil

For the goat's cheese
1 log goat's cheese
(approximately 250g)
75g parmesan cheese

The red onion tarte tatin

Pre-heat the oven to 160°C. Peel and halve the red onions; place on a baking tray and drizzle with olive oil and seasoning. Roast for c.15 mins or until cooked.

While the onions are in the oven, put the sugar and water into a heavy-bottomed pan on a medium heat. When the sugar starts to turn a golden caramel colour around the edges, keep the caramel moving in order to evenly distribute the heat. Pour in the cream and stir. Add the diced butter piece by piece, whisking it in thoroughly. Add rosemary and cook for a further 2 mins.

Remove the caramel from the heat. Put a little into the bottom of each mould and press the red onion into the caramel, with the flat side facing down. Cut 6 puff pastry lids the same size as the mould and put one on top of each onion. Brush the pastry with egg wash and bake at 190°C for c.15 mins.

The shallot purée

Sweat the shallots, garlic and thyme with butter in a pan over a medium heat, until translucent. Cover the shallots with a half milk/half cream mix and cook until the shallots are soft. Separate the shallots from the liquid. Blend. Whilst the machine is running, slowly add the milk/cream mix until you have a thick purée. Season to taste. Pass through a fine sieve and set aside.

The baby onions

Peel, place in a bowl. Pour boiling water on top and cover with cling film; leave it to stand for 5 mins. Remove from the water and dry. Add some butter and oil to a hot pan, add baby onions and pan fry until golden.

The goat's cheese

Cut a log of goat's cheese to make 2 cm thick disks. Remove the outer rind to form a circle. Coat both sides of the disk with grated parmesan and grill until the parmesan bubbles.

To serve

Put some shallot purée on a plate in a teardrop shape. Put the tarte tatin and place on the plate with the goat's cheese. Scatter the baby onions over the purée; serve with a rocket salad.

Roast grouse with foie gras butter, game chips & bread sauce

Serves: 4

Preparation time: 1 hr 30 mins

For the roast grouse

4 whole grouse
½ bunch of thyme

For the croûtons

A slice of white bread (no crust)
Clarified butter

For the foie gras butter

100g foie gras lobe, de-veined
300g butter
2 sprigs of thyme
Splash of brandy
Salt and pepper

For the bread sauce

½ loaf of white bread (no crusts)
500ml full fat milk
2 tbsp double cream
½ white onion
2 cloves
1 bay leaf
½ blade mace
30g butter
Grated nutmeg to taste
Salt and pepper

For the game chips

1 large chipping potato

The grouse

Pre-heat the oven to 200°C. Season the grouse with salt and pepper. Stuff the birds with thyme. Heat a pan with a small amount of oil. Seal the bird until golden all the way around; roast for 20-40 mins.

The croûtons

Use a cutter to cut 4 circles, 5 cm in diameter, from a slice of white bread. Pan fry in clarified butter until golden brown on both sides.

The foie gras butter

Beat the butter until soft. Pan fry the foie gras until it is golden. Add thyme and brandy; flambé the brandy; then place the foie gras in a food processor. Blend until smooth; season to taste. Lay out a piece of cling film and place the butter onto it. Fold the cling film over the butter and roll into a ballotine. Leave in the fridge to chill.

The bread sauce

Dice the bread into 1 cm cubes; stud the onion with cloves and bay leaves. Pour milk and cream into a saucepan with the onion, and heat gently until almost boiling. Remove from the heat and cover with cling film; stand for 15 mins for the ingredients to infuse. Sieve the milk and put onto a low heat. Add the bread, stirring occasionally, until the sauce thickens; season to taste. Add the butter and nutmeg.

The game chips

Peel the potato and slice as thinly as possible. Deep fry the slices until golden brown.

To serve

Place the whole grouse onto a plate. Remove the cling film, slice the foie gras butter, and place the butter onto the croûton. Serve the bread sauce on one side. Finish with a bundle of watercress and the game chips.

DESSERTS

Banana bavarois with chocolate marquise, banana cake crumb & peanut flapjack

Preparation time: 5 hrs

Serves: 8

For the banana bavarois

1½ large bananas (chopped)
60g caster sugar
Banana liqueur to taste
300ml double cream
3 egg yolks
2 sheets large bronze gelatine

For the chocolate marquise

4 eggs
2 egg yolks
125g butter
200g dark chocolate

For the chocolate marquise sponge

2 eggs
85g caster sugar
65g self-raising flour
21g cocoa powder

For the banana cake crumb

50g butter
80g caster sugar
1 egg
1 overripe banana
110g self raising flour
½ tsp baking powder
2 tbsp milk
1 tbsp banana liqueur
20g crushed walnuts

For the peanut flapjack

62g oats
32g caster sugar
32g butter
60g lightly toasted peanuts

Caramelised banana

1 large banana
15g icing sugar

The banana bavarois

Put 10g sugar into a heavy-based pan and put on a medium heat; once the sugar starts to caramelise, add the banana. Stir the banana into the sugar, add 100ml of double cream and banana liqueur. Remove from heat and add the mixture to a food processor. Blend until you have a purée. Set aside.

Soak the gelatine leaves in cold water until soft; set aside. Heat 200ml double cream in a saucepan until just short of boiling. Pour the heated cream over the egg and sugar mix; put the mix back into the pan. Heat gently, stirring to keep the mix moving all the time, until it starts to thicken into a custard. Once thickened, remove the gelatine from the cold water, squeeze out any excess, add to the custard and stir until the gelatine has completely dissolved. Remove from the heat and pass through a fine sieve.

Add the banana purée to the custard and mix thoroughly. Pour the mix into moulds and put in the fridge to set. This will take approximately 4 hrs depending on the size of mould used.

The chocolate marquise

Melt the chocolate and butter together in a heavy-based pan. Meanwhile, add the eggs and egg yolks together in a bowl, whisking until they form stiff peaks. Once the chocolate and butter mixture has completely melted, fold it into the egg mix.

Line a flat baking tray with baking parchment. Whisk eggs and sugar together. Sift the self-raising flour together with the cocoa and slowly add the dry ingredients to the egg mixture. Once all the ingredients are combined, pour into the baking tray and bake at 170°C for roughly 12-15 mins. Once cooked, remove from the baking tray and lay out on a cooling rack. Once cool, cut into pieces that fit the mould you are using.

To assemble the marquise

Lay out some cling film and sprinkle a little water on top (this will help prevent it from sticking to your mould). Line your mould with the cling film, making sure it is tucked into every corner. Put the chocolate mix into the mould, filling it to half way. Place a layer of sponge onto the chocolate mix, and then fill the rest of the mould with more chocolate mix. Once the mould is full, cover and put into the fridge to set (c.20 mins). When set, cut into pieces of the size and shape you want.

The banana crumb

Preheat the oven to 180°C. Lightly grease a flat baking tray and cover the bottom with baking parchment. Put all the ingredients into a mixing bowl and thoroughly mix. Put the mixture into the baking tray. Bake for c.15 mins. Once cool enough remove from the tray and break it up with your hands into rough crumbs. Set aside until needed.

The peanut flapjack

Preheat the oven to 160°C. Toast the oats and peanuts under a grill on a flat tray. Mix butter and sugar, then melt in a pan over a low heat. Once melted stir in the oats and peanuts. Lie out on a shallow baking tray and bake for 4 mins at 180°C.

The caramelised banana

Coat the bananas with the icing sugar. Gently torch the bananas until the sugar caramelises. This can be done under a grill.

To serve

Place the chocolate marquise on to a plate. Arrange the banana bavarois so they are at a slight angle to the marquise. Sprinkle the banana cake crumb and the peanut flapjack around the plate. Place the caramelised banana at intervals around the plate and serve.

Steamed orange pudding with vanilla ice cream

Serves: 6 individual puddings

Preparation time: 45 mins (plus freezing time for the ice cream)

For the puddings

170g unsalted butter
520g caster sugar
Zest and juice of 6 oranges
1 orange, peeled and sliced
3 eggs
170g self raising flour
350ml water

For the ice cream

250ml double cream
375ml whole milk
125g caster sugar
7 egg yolks
2 vanilla pods

The pudding

Beat together the butter, 170g sugar and the zest of 3 oranges until light and fluffy. Add 2 tbsp of orange juice followed by the eggs; beat the mixture well, until all the ingredients are combined. Fold in the flour and salt, followed by the juice of 3 oranges, until the batter has a soft, dropping consistency. Place the remaining sugar and water in a pan and bring to the boil. Add the juice and zest of the remaining oranges and boil until there is a thick syrup in the bottom of the pan.

Line the pudding basins and place a slice of the peeled orange at the bottom of each basin with two tbsp of the orange syrup. Then fill each mould two-thirds full (the pudding will expand when it cooks). Cover with a disc of parchment and then a square of foil, tucking the foil around the rim of the basin to seal. Place in a bain marie, cover with foil and cook in the oven at 190°C for 1 hr.

The ice cream

Heat the milk, cream and vanilla in a heavy saucepan over a high heat. When boiling, remove from the heat and leave to infuse for 30 mins. Beat the egg yolks and sugar in a bowl. Pour the infused milk through a sieve into the bowl and stir as you go. Leave to cool and once completely cold, churn in an ice cream machine until thickened, then decant into a clean container and place in the freezer.

To serve

Turn out the pudding on to a plate. Place a scoop of the vanilla ice cream and drizzle with the remaining orange syrup.

Cheesecake with cherry jellies, cherry gel, almond brittle, yogurt & chocolate soil

Serves: 3

Preparation time: 3 hrs (plus setting time)

For the cheesecake

75g dark chocolate
125g cream cheese
62g sugar
1 egg
1 gelatine leaf
200ml double cream
40g digestive biscuits
10g unsalted butter

For the cherry jelly

35 cherries
150ml water
1 gelatine leaf
50g sugar

For the cherry gel

300g cherries
80ml water
1 clove
1 star anise
100g sugar
14g agar agar

For the almond brittle

140g sugar
60g flaked almonds

For the chocolate soil

150ml water
150g sugar
60g chocolate (melted)

For the yogurt

300g Greek yogurt
80g sugar
100ml whole milk

The cheesecake base

Crush the biscuits in a mixing bowl, and add the chocolate pieces. Melt the butter over a low heat and then add the biscuit mix. Line the bottom of your mould with cling film and press the mix into the bottom making sure it is compacted. Put into the fridge and leave to chill.

The cheesecake

Soak the gelatine leaf in cold water. Whisk the egg yolk, sugar and cream cheese together. In separate bowls, whisk the egg whites and cream to soft peaks. Melt the chocolate over a bain marie and melt the soaked gelatine in a warm pan; then mix the melted chocolate and gelatine into the cream cheese mix. Fold in the cream and the egg white. Put the mixture into a piping bag and pipe on top of the biscuit base. Leave to set.

The cherry jelly

Soak the gelatine leaf in cold water until soft. Put the cherries, water and sugar into a saucepan, and cook over a medium heat until the cherry flavour has infused (taste it to check!). Add the soaked gelatine to the cherry mixture. Pass the liquid through a sieve. Pour on top of the cheesecake.

The cherry gel

Put the cherries, water, sugar, clove and star anise into a saucepan and cook over a medium heat until the cherries are soft. Add the agar agar. Remove from the heat and blend until smooth. Pass through a sieve and allow to set. Once set blend with a small amount of water until it reaches a gel consistency. Put into a squeeze bottle and set aside.

The almond brittle

Heat the sugar in a heavy-based pan over a low flame, until you have a light caramel; add the flaked almonds. Remove from the heat and pour onto a silicone mat; allow to cool. Put the mixture into a blender and make into a fine dust. Put the dust on to a silicone mat; bake at 180°C for 3 mins; remove from the oven, and leave to cool. When cool, break into pieces.

The chocolate soil

Bring the water and sugar to the boil in a saucepan, and then take it to 140°C (use a sugar thermometer). As soon as it reaches 140°C, remove from the heat and add the chocolate, mixing very quickly until it turns into a crumb. Remove from the pan and let it cool.

The yogurt

Mix the yogurt and sugar together then add the milk. Pour the mixture into an espuma gun and leave until needed. If an espuma is not available, use high quality Greek yogurt.

To serve

Place the cheesecake to one side of the plate and poke in bits of the almond brittle. Scatter the chocolate soil around half of the plate. Place dots of the cherry gel around the soil. If you are using an espuma gun, shake it well and gently press the trigger, spraying yogurt foam on the part of the plate not covered by the chocolate soil. Else, spoon the Greek yogurt onto the plate.

Sticky toffee pudding with butterscotch sauce & malt ice cream

Serves: 6

Preparation time: 1 hr 30 mins (plus freezing time for the ice cream)

For the sticky toffee pudding

330g dates
½ tbsp bicarbonate of soda
120g unsalted butter
350g light brown sugar
3 eggs
350g self-raising flour
10ml vanilla essence

For the butterscotch sauce

160ml double cream
155g brown sugar
50g unsalted butter

For the ice cream

250ml double cream
375ml milk
125g caster sugar
7 egg yolks
100ml malt extract

The sticky toffee pudding

Place the dates in a saucepan and just cover with water. Bring to the boil and stir in the bicarbonate of soda; this will cause the water to foam. Put the pan on one side to cool. Cream together the butter, sugar and vanilla until pale. Beat in the eggs, one at a time, then slowly add the date mixture. Gently fold in the flour, making sure not to knock the air out of the mix. Pour into a baking tray and bake at 180°C for 25 mins.

The butterscotch sauce

Melt the butter in a pan and add the sugar. Pour in the cream, stirring constantly, and bring the mix to the boil. Simmer for 5 mins and remove from heat.

The ice cream

Heat the milk and cream in a heavy saucepan over a high heat. When boiling, remove from the heat. Beat the egg yolks and sugar together in a bowl. Pour the infused milk through a sieve into the bowl and stir as you go. Add the malt extract to taste. Leave to cool and once completely cold churn in an ice cream machine until thickened, then decant into a clean container and place in the freezer.

To serve

Turn out the puddings and place in a bowl. Pour the butterscotch sauce over and top with the malt ice cream.

Pistachio sponge with blackberry coulis & rosewater Chantilly

Serves: 8

Preparation time: 45 mins (plus cooling time)

For the pistachio sponge

4 eggs
250g caster sugar
125ml oil (½ olive, ½ vegetable)
Zest of 2 oranges
250g pistachio nuts, blended
70g polenta
125g plain flour
2 tsp baking powder

For the rosewater Chantilly cream

250ml cream
60g icing sugar
Rose essence to taste

For the meringue

3 egg whites
120g sugar
40ml water

For the blackberry coulis

250g blackberries
50g caster sugar
½ tsp vanilla extract
Fresh blackberries to garnish

The pistachio sponge

Whisk the eggs, sugar and oil together until pale and fluffy. Fold in the flour, polenta, baking powder, pistachios and orange zest. Bake at 170°C in a lined baking tray, for 15-20 mins. Leave to cool. When the sponge is completely cold, cut in half width ways then fill with the rosewater cream. Sandwich the sponge back together.

The rosewater Chantilly cream

In a bowl, whisk the cream to soft peaks, then whisk in the icing sugar and rose water until the mix forms stiff peaks.

The meringue

Combine the sugar and water in a small pan over a low heat. Do not stir; swirl the pan over the heat to dissolve the sugar completely. Once the sugar has dissolved, increase the heat. In a bowl, whisk the egg whites until stiff peaks are formed. Whilst continuously whisking, pour the hot sugar syrup in a thin stream over the fluffed egg whites, and continue beating until the bowl feels cold to the touch. Using a palette knife spread the meringue over the top of the pistachio sponge, making stippled peaks all over its top.

The blackberry coulis

Put the blackberries and sugar into a small pan with 100ml water. Bring to the boil and simmer for 5 mins. Stir in the vanilla, remove from the heat and allow to cool a little. Tip the contents of the pan into a blender and blend to a purée; finally strain through a sieve, rubbing it through with the back of a spoon.

To serve

10-15 mins before serving, gently burn the top of the meringue with a blow torch to give a toasted marshmallow flavour. Leave it to stand for 10 mins. Cut the sponge into 8 equal sized rectangles. Serve with the coulis, fresh blackberries and any extra cream.

Warm ginger cake with liquorice ice cream & Amaretti biscuits

Serves: 6

Preparation time: 1 hr 45 mins (plus freezing time for the ice cream)

For the ginger cake

125g unsalted butter
125g muscovado sugar
55g treacle
190g plain flour
2 ½ tsp ground ginger
2 ½ tsp ground cinnamon
1 egg
30g stem ginger
150ml whole milk
1 tsp bicarbonate of soda

For the butterscotch sauce

160ml double cream
150g brown sugar
150g unsalted butter
½ tsp ground ginger

For the Amaretti biscuits

340g ground almonds
340g caster sugar
4 egg whites
30ml Amaretto liquor

For the ice cream

250ml double cream
375ml milk
125g caster sugar
7 egg yolks
Liquorice essence to taste

The ginger cake

Preheat the oven to 180°C. Gently heat the butter, sugar and treacle in a pan until smooth. In a large bowl, sieve together the flour and the spices. Pour in the treacle mix and combine. Finely chop the stem ginger and add to the mix. Beat in the eggs one at a time. Warm the milk gently in a saucepan, add the bicarbonate of soda and let it steam a little. Add to the ginger cake mix and stir until well combined. Bake in a oven proof dish for c. 45 mins.

The butterscotch sauce

Place all ingredients in a pan and bring to the boil; simmer for 5 mins until emulsified.

The Amaretti biscuits

Whisk the egg whites until they stand in stiff peaks. Gently whisk in the sugar, and fold the ground almonds and Amaretto into the mix, making sure it is well combined. Pipe the batter into your desired shape on a lined tray. Bake at 170°C for 10-15 mins.

The ice cream

Heat the milk and cream in a saucepan over a high heat. Beat the egg yolks and sugar together in a bowl. Pour the liquid through a sieve into the bowl and stir as you go. Add the liquorice essence to taste. Leave to cool and once completely cold churn in an ice cream machine until thickened, then decant into a clean container and place in the freezer.

To serve

Place the ginger cake in a bowl and pour over the ginger butterscotch sauce. Add a scoop of liquorice ice cream and top with crushed Amaretti biscuits. Serve whole biscuits alongside if you wish.

Reform Trifle

Serves: 6

Preparation time: 1 hr 45 mins

For the crème anglaise

500ml double cream
1 vanilla pod
6 egg yolks
100g sugar
25g corn flour

For trifle sponge

375g butter
375g sugar
6 eggs
375g self raising flour
2 tsp vanilla essence

Fruit compôte

340g of frozen raspberries
100g caster sugar
4 tbsp water

For the Chantilly cream

200ml of double cream
Icing sugar to taste

To serve

Sherry to taste (optional)
Summer berries
Chocolate shavings

The crème anglaise

Bring the cream to the boil with the split vanilla pods. In a separate bowl whisk together the egg yolks, sugar and corn flour. Once the cream is boiling, pour half over the egg yolk mix and stir until smooth, return the mix back to the pan and cook out until thickened. Strain and leave to cool.

The trifle sponge

Beat the butter, sugar and vanilla essence together until light and fluffy. Add the eggs one by one. Then fold in the flour. Bake at 170°C for approximately 35-45 mins or until golden brown and spongey to touch. When cool, cut the sponge into small cubes.

The fruit compôte

Combine the raspberries, sugar and water in a small saucepan; bring to the boil and leave for 5 mins. Reduce heat to low; simmer the mixture until thick (c.10 mins).

The Chantilly cream

Whip the cream into soft peaks. Add the icing sugar to taste and put into a piping bag.

To serve

Combine the fruit compôte with the sponge mix and add your desired amount of sherry. Leave to marinade for 15 mins. Spoon the mixture into glasses or a large bowl. Cover with a thick layer of the crème anglaise. Pipe the cream on top. Garnish with summer berries and chocolate shavings.

Blueberry & lime tart with Italian meringue

Serves: 6

Preparation time 1 hr 45 mins

For the tart

Sweet pastry (see p. 114)
600g blueberries
300ml soured cream
2 eggs
100g caster sugar
½ tsp cinnamon
½ tsp all spice
Zest and juice of 1 lime
25ml Drambuie
A pinch of salt

For the meringue

60ml egg white
120g sugar
40ml water

To serve

White chocolate shavings

The tart

Pre-heat the oven to 200°C. Line a tart case with grease proof paper. Lightly flour the work surface and roll out sweet pastry to roughly 4mm thickness; then line the tart case with pastry. Trim the edges and let it rest in the fridge for 10 mins. Prick the bottom of the pastry and blind bake for 15 mins. As soon as you remove the pastry from the oven, wash the bottom of the tart case with beaten egg; this will prevent it from absorbing moisture from your filling.

Lower the temperature of the oven to 170°C. Beat 2 eggs and whisk in the caster sugar, cinnamon, all spice, lime, salt and Drambuie. Once thoroughly mixed, slowly whisk in the soured cream. Scatter 200g of blueberries across the bottom of your tart case. Pour the mixture over the blueberries and bake the tart in the oven for 15-20 mins. Once cooked, set aside to cool.

The meringue

In a small pan over a low heat, combine the sugar and water until the sugar is completely dissolved; do not stir it – instead, swirl the pot over the heat to dissolve the sugar completely and stop it sticking. Once the sugar is dissolved, increase the heat and bring to 120°C; use a sugar thermometer for accuracy.

In a bowl, whisk the egg whites until stiff peaks are formed. Pour the hot sugar syrup in a thin stream over the beaten egg whites, whisking continuously. Keep beating until the bowl feels cold to the touch. Put the meringue into a piping bag.

To serve

Place a slice of tart onto the plate and pipe the meringue around it and on top. Using a créme brulée torch, lightly toast the meringue. Sprinkle with white chocolate shavings and fresh blueberries.

Chocolate brownie mousse with salted caramel

Serves: 6

Preparation time: 1hr 50 mins

For the brownie

2 eggs
175g caster sugar
180g dark chocolate
60g milk chocolate
150g unsalted butter
1 tsp vanilla essence
20g cocoa powder
½ tsp baking powder
60g plain flour
100g hazelnuts

For the chocolate cream

400ml double cream
400ml milk
7 egg yolks
100g sugar
500g dark chocolate

For the glaze

75ml water
80g sugar
27g cocoa powder
75ml cream
1½ gelatine leaves
20g dark chocolate

For the salted caramel

120g sugar
90g glucose
200ml double cream
30g unsalted butter (cubed)
50g salt

The brownie

Toast and chop the hazelnuts. In a bowl over a bain marie melt the dark and milk chocolate with the butter until smooth. Whisk the eggs, sugar and vanilla essence in a bowl until light and fluffy. Add the chocolate mix to the eggs and sugar. Fold the flour, cocoa powder and hazelnuts into the mix. Pour into a lined baking tray and cook at 170°C for 15mins.

The chocolate cream

Whisk the egg yolks and sugar together in a bowl until light and fluffy. Bring the milk and cream to the boil in a saucepan. Once the milk is boiling, pour 1/3 of it onto the sugar and egg yolks, whisking to combine; return the mixture to the pan and cook for 2 mins over a medium heat. Break the chocolate into rough pieces in a separate bowl; pour the hot liquid over the chocolate; whisk until the chocolate is completely melted.

Before pouring the chocolate on top of the brownie, push the sides of the brownie to the edge of the tray to seal the edges. Pour on the chocolate cream mix and bake at 150°C for 15-20 mins, and allow to cool.

The glaze

Soak the gelatine in a bowl of cold water until soft. Boil the water and sugar together for 2-3 mins; add cocoa powder and cream and bring back to the boil. Take the pan off the heat and add the soaked gelatine leaves, followed by the chocolate. When the chocolate has melted, strain the mixture to remove any lumps. Once it is totally smooth, pour over the brownie mousse.

The salted caramel

Put the sugar and glucose in a deep pan with enough water to make a sand-like texture. Cook over a low heat until the sugar turns to a golden caramel colour. Keep the pan on the heat and add the cream in three stages, whisking constantly. *Continued on facing page.*

Vanilla panacotta with raspberry compôte & sablé biscuits

Serves: 6

Preparation time: 45 mins (plus at least 4 hrs for the setting of the panacotta)

For the panacotta

500ml double cream
75g icing sugar
2 vanilla pods
1 ½ gelatine leaves, soaked

For the compôte

2 punnets of raspberries
200ml raspberry purée
100g sugar

For the sablé biscuits

120g flour
40g icing sugar
80g butter
Pinch salt
1 egg yolk
20g corn flour

The panacotta

Start by soaking the gelatine in cold water. Heat the cream and vanilla pods in a pan until just boiling. Remove from the heat and stir in the sugar. Cover with cling film and stand for 30 mins to allow the vanilla to infuse. Put a small amount of the cream onto a low heat. Squeeze any excess water out of the gelatine and add it to the cream on the stove. Keep stirring until the gelatine has completely dissolved, and then add the gelatine mix to the rest of the cream. Strain the whole mix through a sieve to remove the vanilla pods and pour into small glasses or jars. Leave to set in the fridge.

The compôte

Heat the sugar and raspberry purée in a pan and boil for c.5 mins to reduce slightly. Remove from the heat and stir in the raspberries.

The sablé biscuits

Place all ingredients except the egg yolk in a mixing bowl and combine to a breadcrumb consistency. Then add the egg yolk and knead together to a smooth dough. Roll the dough out on a lightly floured surface and bake at 170°C for 10-15 mins.

To serve

Top the panacottas with the raspberry compôte and serve with sablé biscuits on the side.

Continued from previous page If the caramel begins to solidify, don't worry; it will melt when the temperature increases again. Keep whisking until the mixture is smooth and all the cream is mixed. Remove the pan from the heat; add the cubed butter a bit at a time. Once all the butter is stirred in thoroughly, add the salt.

To serve

Liberally smear the salted caramel across the plate and place the brownie on top.

BASIC RECIPES

Vegetable stock

2 large carrots, sliced
3 sticks of celery, sliced
1 leek, sliced
1 large onion, sliced
½ bulb of garlic
Splash of vegetable oil
5 black peppercorns
Pinch of coriander seeds
1 bay leaf
Salt to taste
4 litres of water

In a large pot heat the oil until hot but not smoking. Sweat the onion and garlic until translucent (c.5 mins). Add the rest of the ingredients except the water and continue to cook. When the fragrances start to come out of the pot, pour in the water and simmer for c.35 mins. Pass through a fine sieve.

Chicken stock

1½ kg chicken bones
1 carrot, roughly chopped
1 onion, quartered
1 stalk celery, roughly chopped
6 black peppercorns
1 dried bay leaf
3 fresh parsley stalks
1 sprig of fresh thyme
2 tbsp of vegetable oil
4 litres of water

Roast the bones at 180°C until golden brown. In a stock pan sweat the onion until translucent. Add the remaining vegetables and herbs and cook for a further 5 mins. Drain the fat from the roasting tray and add the chicken bones to the stock pan. Cover the bones with water and simmer. Leave for c.3-4 hrs, skimming any fats or grease from the surface of the stock. Pass the stock through a fine sieve, or muslin cloth.

Fish stock

1kg white fish bones
(flat fish is preferable)
2 sticks celery
1 fennel bulb
1 onion, sliced
1 lemon, sliced
120ml dry white wine
4 litres water
4 sprigs of thyme
2 tbsp vegetable oil

Soak the fish bones in water to remove the blood. Chop. Heat the oil in a large pot. Add vegetables and gently cook for c.5 mins. Once translucent, add your chopped fish bones and continue to cook without browning for c.5 mins. Deglaze the pan with the white wine and reduce slightly. Add the water and simmer gently for c.20 mins. Remove from the stove. Add the coriander seeds, lemon and thyme. Cover in cling film. Leave to stand for 10 mins. Pass the stock through a fine sieve and muslin cloth if to hand.

Brown veal stock

1kg veal bones
2 onions, quartered
2 carrots, halved
4 sticks of celery
½ leek, chopped
½ bulb garlic
5 sprigs thyme
4 tbsp tomato purée
Splash of oil
5 litres of water
5 black peppercorns
100ml red wine

Roast the veal bones in the oven at 180°C until golden brown. In a large pan heat the oil until almost smoking and add the onions; caramelise until golden. Add the rest of the vegetables, herbs and tomato purée, continue to cook for 5 mins. Deglaze with the red wine and reduce slightly. Remove the bones from the oven; drain off all the fat and add to the pan; fill with water and bring to the boil. Skim off unwanted foam and fat from the surface. Simmer for at least 12 hrs skimming as often as possible. Top up with water when necessary. After 12 hrs remove from the heat and pass through a fine sieve or muslin cloth.

Red wine reduction & jus

1 litre red wine
4 banana shallots, sliced
2 tbsp tomato purée
6 sprigs of thyme
4 cloves garlic
1 litre veal stock

Red wine reduction

In a saucepan, sweat off the shallots and garlic for c.5 mins until slightly golden. Add the tomato purée and cook out, stirring continuously as the purée will burn easily. Add the red wine and thyme. Simmer to reduce the liquid to a sticky glaze.

Red wine jus

Add 1 litre of veal stock to the red wine reduction. Bring to the boil and reduce until the liquid can coat the back of a spoon. Pass through a fine sieve.

Club dressing

5 tbsp white wine vinegar
4 tbsp walnut oil
8 tbsp olive oil
1 tsp Dijon mustard
1 tsp mustard powder
Sea salt and white pepper
115ml crème fraîche

Whisk or blend the Dijon mustard, mustard powder and white wine vinegar to form an emulsion. Slowly drip in the olive oil; continuing to blend the ingredients. (If the oil is added too quickly, the mix will split). Mix in the crème fraîche and season to taste.

Brioche rolls

Preparation time: Brioche rolls need at least 12 hrs to rest in the fridge so make the dough the night before they are required.

20ml milk
500g strong flour
60g caster sugar
8g salt
3 eggs
20g yeast
300g butter

Heat the milk until tepid and add the yeast; leave to ferment until foamy. Sieve the flour, salt, sugar into a mixing bowl; add the eggs and milk/yeast mix to form a smooth dough. Add the butter to the dough and mix for c.10 mins. Put the dough into a bowl, cover and leave in the fridge for 12 hrs. The dough should now be stiff and easily shaped. Mould the dough pieces into balls or your desired shape. Leave the brioche in a warm place to rise for 1hr. Pre-heat the oven to 200°C. Brush the brioche with the egg wash and bake for c.20 mins. Leave to cool.

Focaccia dough

Preparation time: 1 hour
(plus proving time)

1½ kg white bread flour
1 litre water
35g fresh yeast
35g table salt
50ml olive oil
Fine sea salt
2 sprigs of rosemary (chopped)

Make a starter dough by whisking 750g of flour with the water and the yeast to form a loose batter. Leave to ferment until it doubles in size. Slowly combine the remaining flour and salt with the starter dough and place into a well-oiled bowl. Cover with cling film. Leave in a warm place until the dough doubles in size. Knock back the dough; stretch out into a square, tuck the edges under and knead for 5 mins. Stretch the dough out to cover a square baking tray and leave to prove again before baking. Pre-heat the oven to 220°C. Drizzle the loaves with any remaining oil, sprinkle with fine sea salt and rosemary. Bake in the oven for 20 mins.

Wholemeal bread

Preparation time: 1 hr (plus proving time)

375g wholemeal bread flour
375g white bread flour
20g honey
20g caster sugar
20g salt
75g softened butter
50ml olive oil
375ml tepid water
20g fresh yeast

Add all the ingredients except the yeast and water to a mixing bowl. Dissolve the yeast into the tepid water. Add the water and yeast mixture and work for c.5 mins until it forms a soft smooth dough. Tip out into a floured bowl and leave to prove somewhere warm.

Once the dough has doubled in size, roll the dough into your desired shape. Place onto a tray lined with plenty of semolina or a greased loaf tin. Prove once more until it doubles in size before baking at 180°C for approximately 10 mins for rolls or 30 mins for a loaf.

White bread

Preparation time: 1 hr (plus proving time)

750g white bread flour
20g honey
20g caster sugar
20g salt
75g softened butter
50ml olive oil
375ml tepid water
20g fresh yeast

Add all the ingredients except the yeast and water to a mixing bowl. Dissolve the yeast into the tepid water. Add the water and yeast mixture and work for c.5 mins until it forms a soft smooth dough. Tip out into a floured bowl and leave to prove somewhere warm.

Once the dough has doubled in size, roll the dough into your desired shape. Place onto a tray lined with plenty of semolina or a greased loaf tin. Prove once more before baking at 180°C for approximately 10 mins for rolls or 30 mins for a loaf.

Sweet pastry

500g plain flour
250g butter
125g sugar
2 eggs
1 egg yolk

Beat together the butter and sugar until light and fluffy. Beat in the eggs and the egg yolk, one at a time, until they are fully incorporated into the mixture. Combine the flour until the mixture forms a ball of dough. Knead briefly to make the pastry smooth. Wrap the dough in cling film and rest in the fridge for 30 mins.

This pastry can be frozen.

Short crust pastry

110g plain flour
25g lard
25g butter
Water to bind
Pinch of salt

Using your hands, soften the butter and lard until pliable. Add the flour and salt, gently rub the ingredients together to form a dough; this should take c.10 mins. A small amount of liquid may be required in order to bind the mix together. The pastry should be smooth, without any random lumps of fat or flour. Shape the mix into a ball and wrap in cling film. Leave to rest in the fridge for at least an hour before use.

Pasta recipe

500g 00 flour (pasta flour)
4 eggs
2 egg yolks
Splash of oil

Preparing the dough

Pile the flour on a clean work surface and create a well in the centre. Beat the egg and egg yolks and pour into the well. Gently bring the flour in from the outside and combine until it becomes stiff. When you reach this stage, form the dough into a ball and knead for c.5 mins or until smooth and elastic. Eggs can vary in size and flour can vary in humidity; the dough should not be too wet or dry. Add a touch of water if necessary. Wrap the dough in cling film and leave in to relax for 30 mins.

Rolling the pasta

Divide the pasta into four pieces and cover with a damp tea towel. Flatten out each piece of dough by hand and run through the thickest setting on a pasta machine. Place on a narrower setting and pass the pasta through again. Fold the dough in two and repeat until the dough is smooth. Keep rolling the pasta sheet through the pasta machine, reducing the thickness each time and dusting with flour as you go. Continue until you are down to the desired thickness. For shapes like linguine, tagliatelle and lasagne this is 2mm. (1mm for all folded pasta like ravioli and tortellini).

WINES

Pairing wine with food

The foundation document of the Club records that "there shall be a club for Reformers to be called the Reform Club". The very next sentence reads "Item 1. There shall be a Wine Committee". Wine has occupied a central place in the Club ever since. In the heart of the building, the Central Cellar was conceived as the main wine storage. However, since the introduction of electricity, many of the old coal cellars under the gardens and under Pall Mall are now also used for storing wine.

The Club has, as one would expect, an excellent and plentiful supply of claret – the wine drunk most by Members. In order of consumption, the Club Dry White and the Club Champagne, are also popular. However the wine list covers a very wide range, both in geography and in price, to provide the most appropriate wine for any meal. There are no fixed suppliers; the Club attempts to achieve the best quality at the best price and purchases wine from a number of importers.

Wine tastes have significantly changed since the founding of the Club: Hock is no longer served, and the fortified wines which were so popular in the early years are now distinctly less preferred. In the earliest stock list of the Club, many clarets (known not by the names of the châteaux but by the names of the importers) are clearly prominent.

The following comments by the Club's Cellarmaster, Giovanni de Rose, may be of interest when you choose wines to complement the recipes in this book.

Food and wine are paired to create an intense balance of flavours. When you get it right, this balance results in the most enjoyable dining experience. There are two main ways to pair wine: either by contrast or similarity.

Paring wines by similarity means choosing flavours that are present in both the food and the wine. The best way to describe this is to imagine that the flavours are fighting each other in an even fight. You do not want the flavours over-powering each other. An example of this would be the pairing of a peppery Shiraz with Steak au Poivre.

Pairing by contrast involves thought, particularly about the different characteristics of the wine. Pairing a high acidity wine, like a Chardonnay, with a naturally oily dish such as salmon, results in the crisp freshness of the wine contrasting well with the light oily texture of the fish.

The characteristics of wine

There are five key characteristics to consider when choosing your wines.

Body: the body of a wine can roughly described as full-bodied, medium or light. This characteristic relates to the intensity of the flavour of the wine. A robust full-bodied wine will fill your mouth and explode on your tongue, whereas a light wine has a more delicate flavour.

Complexity: the complexity of wine relates to the number of flavours that can be tasted or smelt. For example, a wine in which you can smell citrus, peach and a subtle hint of spice is a complex wine, especially when compared to a wine in which only citrus can be smelt.

Alcohol and sugar levels: high levels of alcohol in the wine result in a slightly bitter after taste. They are therefore more suited to being paired with a juicier food such as steak. A lower alcohol wine pairs best with food that is less moist, such as pan fried fish or salads. The levels of sugar also directly relate to the sweetness of the wine; a lower alcohol wine tends to be sweeter. Really sweet wines are generally paired with desserts. However, a sweet wine such as Sauternes also works well with cheese and traditionally is served with foie gras.

Tannin: tannin is a textural ingredient which makes wine taste dry. Therefore the more tannins in a wine, the dryer it tastes. Tannin is generally found in red wines, but can be found in white wines which have been aged in wood barrels.

Acidity: a high level of volatile acids results in a sharp, fresh and slightly tart taste. The acidity relates to the region from which the wine comes and the time of year the grapes have been picked. Low acid wines tend to come from countries with warmer weather, such as Australia. Wines with a high acid often come from regions of France or Britain, which have a cooler climate.

Suggested wine pairings: starters

Smoked trout; a white Sauvignon from New Zealand would provide an ideal complement not only to the trout and cucumber, but also to the complex flavours of the horseradish cheesecake.

Salmon jellies; a delicately smoky taste and the texture of silk, to firm, fleshy fish with a tangy, intensive taste makes this dish complementary with a white northern Rhône wine with a lush, soft character. The highly aromatic and fruit-forward nature of the grape allows Viognier to pair well with this dish.

Squash and sheep's curd cannelloni; the gentle acidity and marked fruitiness of a well-balanced Pinot Gris from New Zealand perfectly complements the cannelloni. Grown throughout the country, the New Zealand Pinot Gris has notes of apple, pear, honeysuckle and spice.

Confit duck, cherry & gingerbread; this dish is quite flavoursome and can cope with more powerfully flavoured wine like a Riesling from Germany. The cherry will connect with German Riesling Spätlese. Off-dry Rieslings are also great in mimicking sweetness and would go very well with the gingerbread.

Scallops & leeks; with the subtle, complex flavours of scallops it is important to find a wine that will complement rather than overpower. A crisp, dry, light Sauvignon Blanc from the Loire is a great accompaniment to scallops, with the acidity of the wine cutting through the sweetness of the shellfish and the light fruity hints drawing out the nuances of flavour in the dish.

Veal cushion; veal is often compared to beef but is more delicate in taste, lighter in colour and finer in texture. A Pinot Noir, especially from Burgundy, will match this dish with its red berry touch. Its mild acidity is often just crisp enough to broaden the range of white meat like veal.

Heirloom tomatoes & goat's cheese; Chardonnay from a warmer area such as Chile or Australia has low acidity and reasonably more alcohol. It would balance the acidity of the tomato and goat's cheese.

Wood pigeon; wood pigeon needs a mature but full-flavoured red wine. It would be complemented well with a rich fruit and beautiful floral spice; a wine that while big and bold remains balanced and elegant, such as a Rioja.

Guinea fowl terrine; a slightly hearty flavour makes it ideal to go with Chardonnay from the Mâconnais area in the south of Burgundy. With its fresh floral aromas, the wine shows elegant, rich fruit on the palate which pairs well with this terrine.

Suggested wine pairings: mains

Roast fillet of pork; pork is often quite fatty, and since tannin clashes with fat, a low tannin wine with a fruity flavour of berries such as a Beaujolais from France would be ideal.

Gnocchi with mushroom velouté; this dish would go very well with an Alsace Pinot Blanc from France. It has a certain roundness of flavour, verging sometimes on apparent sweetness because the acidity is relatively low.

Pan fried sea bass; Albariño from Spain or an Alvarinho from Northern Portugal are well balanced wines with good acidity and the right minerality to complement the sea bass.

Hardwick lamb; Salt-marsh lamb, with its slight saltiness and hint of seaweed, together with the mint, calls for a St Julien from Bordeaux. There is a very wide range available depending on budget.

Roast loin of rabbit; its own distinct flavour makes this dish very easily paired with a Côtes de Provence Rosé from the South of France. This beautiful bright and dry wine with an elegant, refreshing taste complements perfectly this dish.

Hake with beetroot & pear; its agreeable texture and light flavour makes this fish a perfect match with a bright and sharp wine like a white Rhône.

Ox cheek ravioli; in the Piedmont region of Italy, it is traditional to pair agnolotti with Barolo. This matches a robust food with a tannic, structured wine with good complexity and a high alcohol level. We therefore recommend a Barolo with our ox-cheek ravioli.

Lamb Cutlets Reform; this original dish by Alexis Soyer has a very complex and rich sauce which requires a full-bodied red wine with dark flavours such as a Cabernet Sauvignon from Bordeaux.

Breaded lamb breast & sweetbreads; lamb is a lot more delicate in flavour than most beef, so generally you can select lighter wine. A wine from the North of Rhône starts with a fruity flavour and then finishes in a blend of soft tannins and balanced acidity which balances the lamb.

Cod cheeks; lightly oaked Chablis (France) is a touch austere and has a beautiful fresh minerality which makes this wine perfect with this dish.

Sea trout; trout has an excellent firm texture and a good, if delicate, flavour which needs a wine from the South of Italy like Falaghina. The balance of crispness and texture means this wine complements a wide range of food.

Red onion tarte tatin; the sweetness of the caramelised shallots in this tart requires a ripe, aromatic white like a Sauvignon Blanc from Chile. Its freshness and balance stand out in particular.

Roast grouse; we would normally recommend a claret, but the foie gras butter introduces a complexity of taste, opening up more possibilities. Should you wish a claret, a Lalande de Pomerol would go well; but you may wish to try a South African red from the Cape.

Suggested wine pairings: desserts

Banana bavarois; a complex dessert such as this, with many different flavours, needs a wine with some sharpness and which is not over sweet. We recommend a Muscat.

Steamed orange pudding; matching for similarity, a Sauternes – with its range of flavours which include orange skin and dried peel – would work well with the steamed orange pudding.

Cheesecake with cherry jellies; in this case we suggest matching the richness of the dessert with a rich wine. The dessert has many different textures, and these will go well with a Sauternes, a multilayered wine with many different flavours supporting those of the dessert.

Sticky toffee pudding; this is very sweet and calls for something full in the mouth with a very rich texture. The dark, rich, nuttiness – with a hint of salt – of oloroso sherry both complements and cuts through the pudding.

Pistachio sponge; Sauternes, which has already been recommended for the cheesecake, is not a straightforward wine. Its complex, multi-aspected nature would well match both the blackberry and the pistachio in this dish.

Warm ginger cake; combining ginger, liquorice, and almonds produces a dessert with a wide range of contrasting flavours and textures. The wine should not attempt to introduce further complexity, but should be simple and clean. A Muscat would be appropriate.

Reform Trifle; this dessert has been on the Club menu for a long time. Many years of experience have shown that Members prefer two contrasting wines to go with it: either a rich, complex dessert wine (such as a Sauternes) or something more simple, light and direct such as a chilled Gamay (Beaujolais).

Blueberry & lime tart; this is a dessert where it is better to complement than contrast. A Muffato from Umbria/Tuscany has complexity, intensity and long length and a smokey note. It has flavours of tropical fruit, dried fruit and figs. It would be an excellent accompaniment to the tart.

Chocolate brownie mousse; in France, dark chocolate desserts are often paired with red wine. The addition of salted caramel here makes the choice slightly more difficult, but this dessert cries out for a half bottle of a decent Margaux.

Vanilla panacotta; this is very rich; the combination of panacotta, compôte and sablé needs something equally rich and complex but which at the same time has a refreshing mouth feel. A good, well chilled ice wine would provide an elegant and flavoursome complement which is sweet enough to match the dessert, but not so sweet as to be overwhelming.

FURTHER INFORMATION

Head Chefs of the Reform Club 1836–2014

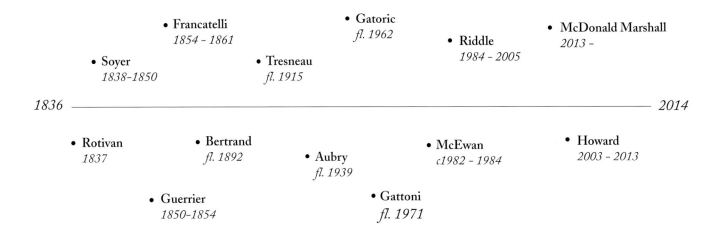

Francatelli
1854 - 1861

Gatoric
fl. 1962

McDonald Marshall
2013 -

Soyer
1838–1850

Tresneau
fl. 1915

Riddle
1984 - 2005

1836 ————————————————————————— *2014*

Rotivan
1837

Bertrand
fl. 1892

Aubry
fl. 1939

McEwan
c1982 - 1984

Howard
2003 - 2013

Guerrier
1850-1854

Gattoni
fl. 1971

With thanks to

Prestige Primeurs

Allen's of Mayfair

Aubrey Allen

Huntsham Court Farm

Yorkshire Game Ltd

London Cheese Board Ltd

Daily Fish Supplies Ltd

Wet Fish (UK1) Ltd

The Colchester Oysters Fishery

H Forman's & Son

MSK Ingredients

Town & Country Fine Foods

We particularly want to thank the Secretary of the Club, Crispin Morton; the Assistant Secretary, Paul Austin; and all those who have had to work round us whilst we took *Recipes from the Reform* from conception to fruition.

Glossary

Agar Agar: a thickening agent extracted from seaweed.

A la Carte: 'carte' was originally a French term for a piece of paper or cardboard and later a menu. Today the term means 'according to the menu'.

Al dente: cook so that there is still a bite to the texture of the food.

Bain marie: 1) a hot water bath that is used to keep food warm on the top of a stove; (2) a fairly large pan (or tray) which is partly filled with water used to slowly cook certain types of food such as crème brulées.

Ballotine: from the French 'ballot', meaning bundle. Traditionally refers to a boned leg of chicken or duck, which is then stuffed and tied. The term also refers to the shape, which is similar to that of a sausage.

Beat: to mix ingredients quickly usually involving a whisk so that air is incorporated.

Blanch: to cook very briefly in boiling water

Blind bake: to partially or completely bake a pastry case before filling it.

Brick pastry: brick pastry looks like fine, lacy cloth with a satiny sheen. When fried it is crisper than spring roll pastry and when baked it has a dry, melt-in the-mouth crunchiness, which is better than filo.

Caramelise: to melt either sugar or sugary foods by cooking slowly over low heat until the contents become browned.

Caul fat: a translucent lace of fat, which melts when cooked, providing moisture and flavour. It also holds ingredients together while cooking.

Coagulate: changes to a liquid from a solid state.

Cook out: leave on the heat till any liquids have evaporated.

Confit: to cook something very slowly in fat.

Clarified butter: when all milk solids are removed from butter, it creates a yellow fat which can tolerate a higher temperature than regular butter.

Cream: to mix a softened ingredient, such as butter, alone or with other ingredients, such as sugar, until smooth.

Cut against the grain: to slice meat against the grain makes the meat more tender.

Dash: a small quantity.

De-glaze: to loosen anything left in a pan by adding a liquid, then heating while stirring and scraping the pan.

Dice: chopping ingredients into neat cubes.

Emulsify: to bind liquids that usually do not blend together.

Espuma gun: an espuma gun is commonly used to make foams by making a stock, creating a gel and extruding through the use of a N_2O canister.

Ferment: to bring about a natural chemical change in food, commonly used to describe the action of yeast.

Flambé: to drizzle liquor over a food while it is cooking and igniting the liquor.

Fold: to incorporate one ingredient into another without stirring or beating.

Grease: to lightly coat a pan with some fat to prevent foods from sticking.

Knead: to work dough after blending ingredients, with the palms of your hand, making it smooth and elastic.

Knock-back: the process of removing excess air from dough before it is proved.

Line: to cover the surface of a baking sheet or roasting pan with foil, waxed, or parchment paper to prevent sticking.

Mandolin: a cooking utensil used for slicing.

Pané: to coat in bread crumbs.

Poach: using water or other liquid to gently cook food. The liquid is brought to a simmer and the ingredients are added to the pan.

Prove: the final dough rise step before baking.

Puff pastry: a light, flaky pastry of many thin layers – made by repeatedly rolling and folding the dough with layers of fat, causing it to 'puff up' when baked.

Pulse: a speed on a food processor. Pulsing allows you to keep a better eye on the consistency of the foods inside the processor.

Reduce: to thicken a liquid and concentrate its flavour by simmering.

Red wine jus: a simple French sauce made from reduced stock and wine.

Refresh: to run hot food under cold water or to plunge into cold water to stop the cooking and retain colour.

Sauté: cook briefly over a high heat.

Sear/seal: to brown the surface of meat very quickly in a hot oven or in a pan over high heat on top of the stove to seal in juices.

Season/adjust the seasoning: this generally refers to the adding of salt and pepper.

Skim: to remove surface foam or fat from a liquid.

Strain: to remove solids from liquids by pouring through a colander or sieve.

Sweat: the gentle heating of vegetables in a little oil or butter, with frequent stirring, to ensure that any emitted liquid will evaporate.

Reform Club: Kitchen Brigade, 2014

Back row (left to right)

Brian Dundas

Hadley Reed

Craig McDonald Marshall

Pawel Ozimkiewicz

Angelo Pirodda

Artur Saavedna

Raudy Biset Hernandez

Maurice Loba Kelie

Alex Fulluck

Front row (left to right)

Bevan Roberts

Kate Elliott

Sam Davies

Anna Robinson

Courtney Lee

Lauren Barrett

Amy Crangle

Bashir Moussadek